Art in Commerce
and Industry

art horizons

Art in Commerce and Industry

Robert Clemens Niece

Art Center College of Design
Los Angeles, California

WM. C. BROWN COMPANY PUBLISHERS
Dubuque, Iowa

ART HORIZONS SERIES

Consulting Editor

WILLARD F. WANKELMAN
Bowling Green State University

A growing interest in art and art history is evident today in the United States and has created a need for a new approach in the formulation of classroom teaching materials.

The ART HORIZONS SERIES, designed for introductory courses in art appreciation and art history, transmits the excitement of the subject to the student seeking a liberal education. This series offers both the student and teacher flexibility of subject matter as well as authoritative writing in each topic area. Although the individual titles are self-contained, collectively they cover the major subjects usually discussed in an introductory course.

Copyright © 1968 by
Wm. C. Brown Company Publishers

Library of Congress Catalog Card Number: 67–22711

Printed in U. S. A.

Dedicated to Charles Eames in appreciation of his considerable efforts on behalf of art education.

preface

In a book of this size, written basically to bring the reader into contact with a few of the major areas of applied art and design, it is clear that many areas would, of necessity, be omitted The examples selected were arbitrary, and obviously, for every one chosen dozens of others could have been used as well.

The fields shown are often overlapping, and many designers work quite comfortably in several fields at once. Actually, the professionals who do so are merely demonstrating a principle: that *design* is their field and the various subdivisions are simply different aspects of that field. Advertising, packaging, product design, and the like are so much a part of everyday life that they are often taken for granted, enjoyed or reviled, accepted or rejected, without their design character being discussed, analyzed, or understood. Our true cultural level may be better evaluated by the esthetic standards found in our everyday possessions— our clothes and tools, dishes and cars, furniture and lighting fixtures— than in our monuments and museums.

contents

Figure 1. Lamp by Bill Curry (see also page 44).

1

Introduction

The line that once separated the "fine" arts from the "applied" arts has in recent years grown increasingly fuzzy. The difference between these two areas of human creativity has blurred to the point of invisibility. Ben Shahn, eminent painter and graphic artist, has executed many illustrations for the Columbia Broadcasting System—work used for advertising in CBS radio and television programing. The Olivetti Corporation of Italy has consistently used the work of outstanding artists in their advertising, and sculptor, Marcello Nizzoli, shaped their now classic award-winning typewriters.

The division of art into two distinct fields is mostly academic, a matter of definition without much meaning in today's world. It is certainly true that most of the people who desire to express themselves in some visual way tend toward painting or sculpture while others are more interested in applying the principles on which art is based to immediate areas of everyday concern, such as advertising or industrial design. But the overlap between these two fields should not be ignored as it is considerable.

At home, perhaps while reading this book, look around the room. The chair or sofa on which you sit, the table nearby, the lamp, and other articles are all things that are probably identical with thousands of others manufactured through the use of mass-production techniques. The cost to you would have been considerably higher and the quality would probably have been much lower had preindustrial methods been used in their making.

If you are a person of taste and discrimination, the furnishings in your room will surely reflect that fact, as surely as they will reflect the opposite. For, in the American economy, a wide variety of goods is available to all in every price range to suit almost everyone's needs. The goods that represent the material values of the American way of life are generally the best available to anyone anywhere. In those special areas wherein the products of some other countries have considerable merit (some Swedish glass, some Danish furniture, some Japanese cameras, some Italian typewriters, some British cars), these are also available to the American public, usually at quite reasonable prices. American goods must be sold abroad, thus creating a situation in which import becomes an integral part of the problem of export.

The standard of living in the United States is at once the envy and the despair of the rest of the world. That high level is, at least in part, the result of an attitude, an approach to life, that is similar to that of the artist, designer, or inventor. Nothing is ever quite good enough; everything can be improved upon; never sit still; never be apathetically content with a solution, a product, or an idea. Develop it, refine it, IMPROVE it.

R. Buckminster Fuller, inventor-engineer-thinker, aims for the maximum performance per pound of material invested in a product and, in his geodesic domes, to take one example, extensive ground areas are roofed with incredibly minute quantities and weights of materials. This kind of goal, while seldom so clearly expressed, is at least a peripheral aim of most designers.

A critical attitude toward our environment is developed by an awareness of such goals and points of view. In this book the reader should keep in mind the general attitude just mentioned. While many comments may appear to be very critical of certain design details of a given product it is a criticism that keeps in mind the fact that the object in question is still probably one of the world's best. The intent here is to bring out points that might make the "best" even better.

As a man grows older and, conceivably, wiser, he alters his position on most subjects. He changes his ideas according to his experiences and his accumulation of information. It is not reasonable to expect a creative individual to remain static, not to grow and broaden. His answer to a problem at one point in his life would logically be somewhat different if the question were posed at another time in his career.

A major advantage in this continual realignment of ideas and concepts is that it lends itself to a restatement of the problem each time a solution is required. New and different limitations may be imposed by the designer on his own work and his design responsibility. Self-imposed limitations are vital in a world of great affluence—a world in which it is quite possible to produce almost any product in tremendous quantities without reference at all to the beauty or ugliness of the object—or even whether or not the thing is actually needed at all.

Good design results from a highly developed sense of self-control, self-restraint. Charles Eames once mentioned that Los Angeles is an example of a city built without restraints, either traditional or material. However, there is no implication here that a strait jacket is to be preferred. Guidelines, principles, a well-understood direction—that is what is meant, and what is needed, before good design is possible.

The changes that are occurring in the number of opportunities being given to major design innovators have come about, partly at least, through a change in attitude toward design on the part of businessmen in general. They have become more aware of the effect of esthetics on sales, but even more importantly, of its effect on the lives of people generally. There is today a far greater degree of sophistication and design awareness on the part of business executives, who are often faced with decisions that have a base in both economics and esthetics. Many of these men come out strongly in favor of the esthetic solution when the question is properly stated.

This change in attitude is also a reflection of a major change that is in the process of occurring on the part of the American public. In all facets of life there is a growing desire for better things to be enjoyed in a better environment. This desire is often poorly expressed—even misunderstood—but it does exist and is a force to be acknowledged.

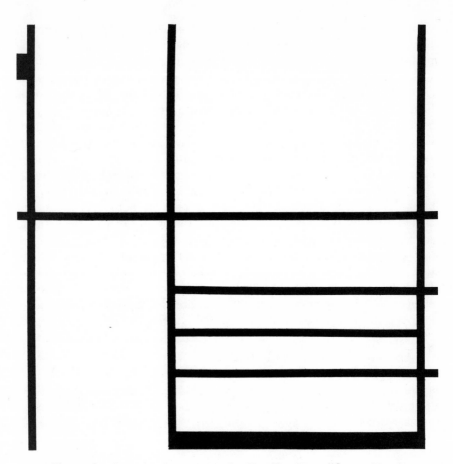

Figure 2. A study of a painting by Piet Mondrian, "Composition in White, Black and Red." 1936. Original in the Museum of Modern Art, New York.

|2

Influences

Today's design grows out of yesterday's events. The ideas and developments of the recent past influences the work currently being completed. Of those complex influences a few have been selected that are, in many ways, still being felt.

ART NOUVEAU

The movement known as Art Nouveau was in evidence during the brief period from 1893 to 1910. Its practitioners broke with the concept of imitating previous styles and developed a unique style of their own. Inspiration was derived from the flowing, twisting forms of growing things: plants, vines, leaves, and flowers. The shapes thus developed were used in everything from furniture to posters, from architecture to glassware.

An iridescent glass developed by Tiffany in the 1880s was used in the manufacture of vases with flowing lines and organic forms. Ignored for a time, these have become collector's items—as have most of the other Art Nouveau objects of that same period. While this style placed emphasis on the odd ideal of growing, plantlike shapes, it nevertheless represented a concept that owed little to the past. In fact it showed a complete preoccupation with its own time.

Exactly why Art Nouveau should undergo a revival is an interesting question, as this style violates almost all rules of common sense and good design. The typefaces are difficult to read; the lighting fixtures are not compatible with studies of the requirements of levels of illumination for various kinds of work around the home; most of the forms look tortured and uncomfortably distorted. Everything is much more difficult to manufacture. The very meaning of the object changes. Something that does a clean and simple job becomes, through the Art

5

Figure 3. One of the many designs of Thonet chairs created through the use of steam-bending techniques applied to beechwood. Many of the original pieces are still in use due to the strength of the light construction. Circa 1875. Client: Thonet. Available: Stendig.

Nouveau treatment, a much-too-precious object. Much ado about very little indeed. Yet such is the period in which we live: excited about strange haircuts one moment, rushing off to teach the Patagonians how to tie a four-in-hand cravat the next. Good design survives somehow—no thanks to Art Nouveau, however.

DE STIJL

A group of Dutch painters organized the De Stijl movement around the time of the first World War—1917 to 1928. It influenced painting, architecture, sculpture, and interior design through its development of overall concepts that could be applied to a variety of art fields and many different types of design problems.

It was characterized by the straight line and the rectangle—by geometrical form. The paintings of Mondrian, van der Leck, van Doesburg, and Huzar; the furniture of Rietveld; the architecture of Oud, Rietveld, van Eestern, and van Doesburg all have this uncompromising character. The attempt of these men was to redefine the role of the artist in the modern world. They placed art in a role based on universal laws of balance and harmony, combined with a return to the basic elements of art. Their paintings were nonobjective—that is, not depictions of objects, scenes, or the visual aspects of the ordinary world around them but, rather, a reliance on a different view of reality. Their vision was an ideal universal harmony, an art of pure relations. The elements were reduced to a minimum. The colors were primary colors: red, yellow, and blue plus black, white, and gray.

The spirit of the modern age, they felt, was best expressed through depersonalization and mathematical precision. The straight line and right angle have long been the marks of man on the face of nature and, with a peculiarly Dutch attitude regarding the place of man and his works in the universe, their goal was a rational art, one rising above the apparent inconsistencies of nature, contrasting with the twisting, undulating forms typical of nature's way of growing. It was a puritan movement deeply rooted in a renunciation of mere depiction of exterior form. Instead, it searched for a way to depict inner, universal harmony. This harmony was the true content of De Stijl art.

In both furniture and architecture the expression of De Stijl became a matter of relating the formal elements of a chair or a building, a reaction against the decorative styles and imitative attitude generally prevalent at the time.

Rietveld's furniture consisted of square sticks used as legs and stretchers, bypassing each other and projecting slightly to emphasize

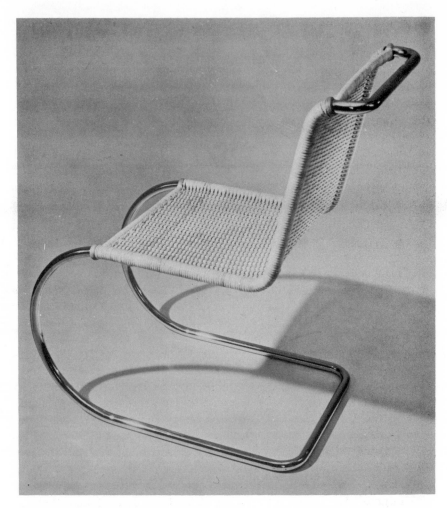

Figure 4. One of the earliest developments of the cantilevered chair with no rear legs. The design creates a flexible action that aids in the occupant's feeling of comfort. Design: Mies van der Rohe. Available: Stendig.

their nonconnected quality. The plain rectangles of plywood used as seats and backs are placed at an angle to the square geometry of the frame.

J. J. P. Oud reached a high point of social architecture in the development of a group of row-house apartments at the Kiefhoek, Rotterdam. The neatness, precision, and clarity of the buildings reflect the anonymous character of modern production. His speech at the opening of the Bauhaus in Dessau was recognized for its enumeration of basic principles of design.

The *Bauhausbücher* series included Mondrian's *Die neue Gestaltung*, Oud's *Holländische Architecktur* and van Doesburg's *Grundbegriffe der neuen Gestaltenden* (Principles of the New Plastic Art).

BAUHAUS

The Bauhaus was a school of design, the first in the world to attempt to come to terms with the machine. Its active life of only some fourteen years (1919 to 1933) packed an incredible amount of intensity into a short, but vital, period. Walter Gropius, the school's director, gathered together a group of people whose influence has, over the years, affected every area of art and design education. The major figures were destined to be unpopular with the Nazi regime that took over Germany in the early 1930s. As a consequence, most of those men left Germany for other, more receptive, countries, several coming to England, then to the United States. Here they continued to practice their professions and most of them performed a vital service by continuing to teach. Laszlo Moholy-Nagy, who had strongly influenced the methods used in teaching the preliminary course, came to Chicago, where he established "The New Bauhaus" that eventually became the Institute of Design of the Illinois Institute of Technology.

Josef Albers, also responsible for the preliminary course at the Bauhaus, taught at Black Mountain College, North Carolina, as well as lecturing at Harvard and at other universities in the United States. Herbert Bayer studied, then taught, at the Bauhaus. His thinking has affected many aspects of graphic design and, since 1938, he has worked in the United States as a leading designer. Marcel Breuer, who developed tubular steel furniture while teaching at the Bauhaus, later taught in the department of architecture at Harvard with Walter Gropius. Lyonel Feininger, painter and graphic artist, taught at the Bauhaus both at Weimar and Dessau. Born in New York, he returned to the United States in 1936. Mies van der Rohe, who kept the Bauhaus going during its last three years despite the Nazis, has, of course,

Figure 5. A side chair of chrome-plated steel tubing with cane on wood frames for seat and back, 1928. Design: Marcel Breuer. Available: Stendig.

established himself as a giant in American architecture since his ar-
rival here in 1937. He headed the School of Architecture at the Armour
Institute (later to become a part of the Illinois Institute of Technology),
where he was Director of Architecture for twenty years. Mies, Frank
Lloyd Wright, and Le Corbusier are usually named as the three great-
est architects of the twentieth century.

The Bauhaus taught basic principles of design that were compatible with the machine age. The products of the workshops looked
like machine-made objects even though this effect was, of necessity, the
result of fine hand craftsmanship. Many of these prototypes were manufactured in quantity by German companies that paid royalties to the
school for their use. Although the products of the workshops were
important because they were among the first to clearly reflect the
possibilities inherent in mass production, the ideas and educational
methods developed in the school affected the world of design even
more. Trained initially by artists and master craftsmen, the students
learned to approach design problems with straightforward simplicity
and creative imagination. They were functionally minded and problem-
oriented. Advanced design became known as "Bauhaus" design throughout Germany and most of Europe.

Many of the ideas, concepts, and methods that, rightly or wrongly,
have become known as Bauhaus concepts have, in recent years, come
in for re-evaluation and a new assessment. Their value is debated, re-
examined, and expanded upon. Their importance is, however, un-
questioned.

OLIVETTI CORPORATION

The Olivetti Corporation was one of the first major corporations
to establish a policy of good design in every aspect of the company's
activities. The design of the products (business machines), the advertising of those products, the showrooms in which the products were
exhibited, the factories in which they were made, even the houses,
apartments, and nurseries of the company's workers were all part of
the assignment given to the best artists, architects, and designers available. Although the creative people who shaped the products, advertising, and buildings were individuals who were not asked to suppress
their own individuality in any way, the one consistent factor in all
these diverse activities was that of quality. Every visual aspect of
Olivetti reflected the highest quality of esthetic understanding.

This sense of quality that came to be associated with the Olivetti
name was an outgrowth of the belief held by Adriano Olivetti that all

Figure 6. *Top:* A lounge chair of tubing and leather in which the body never touches the cold metal but is supported by leather at each point of contact, 1925. Design: Marcel Breuer. Available: Stendig. *Bottom:* An early pivot-back lounge chair with steel frame and arms; seat and back of leather, 1928. Design: Le Corbusier and Perriand.

these issues were of great importance. He felt every contact a person had with the company should be in connection with something that could be easily recognized as outstanding. The typewriters and calculators should not only work wonderfully well but should be as handsome as it was possible to make them. From factories right down to a business card, no detail was too small to be ignored. This policy continues to this day.

IBM

International Business Machines Corporation, much better known as IBM, has a position in the United States economy of considerable importance. Not only is it a corporation of major stature, it is also a leader in the area of design policy as well. The IBM electric typewriter has become a national standard. The recent innovation of the whirling "golf ball" carriageless machine is typical of the creative thinking generally visible in their products. It is the visual aspect of IBM that is of primary concern here and it is in this very area of visual impact that IBM has made an impression on the average American. For several years IBM has followed a corporate design program that includes architecture, product design, and graphic design with a manager in charge of design coordination.

The design consultant responsible for graphics, to take only one part of the total program, is the noted designer Paul Rand. He designs most of the packaging and functions as a consultant to the sizable number of IBM designers who are working in other graphic problem areas. Rand's function is strictly within the area of design. All other matters of materials, sizes, and structure are the responsibility of IBM engineers who develop standards and create new types of construction. The clear sharp typography apparent in IBM packages is typical of Rand's work. These examples help create the overall image of a corporation that knows what it is doing.

THE ARMORY SHOW

It may be impossible to assess with any degree of accuracy the influence of a single factor in a complex situation, yet the influence is undeniably there. A single art exhibition can have considerable effect on the direction of art in an entire country in subsequent years. A case in point: the Armory Show of 1913. This was the first comprehensive showing of examples of modern art in the United States. Well over a thousand items were exhibited, including the work of Cézanne,

Figure 7. A general view of the Armory Show that was so controversial in 1913. Today almost every example shown is considered a classic of modern art. Sculpture in the foreground by Brancusi, Lehmbruck, Maillol and Bernard. A storm of controversy centered around Marcel Duchamp's "Nude Descending the Stairs."

Ingres, Delacroix, Daumier, Renoir, Monet, Matisse, Picasso, Braque, Leger, Pacabia, Kandinsky, Stella, Hopper, Bellows, and Ryder. The reaction of the press was unbelieving ridicule, laughter, and jokes mixed with indignation. Some people were amused, some were angry, many were puzzled, most were frustrated.

Marcel Duchamps' painting, *Nude Descending a Staircase,* became the center of a storm of ridicule and rage. This canvas immediately became a symbol for modern art itself. Years later, after exposure to a great many examples of modern art, the public not only ceased to object to works that are rather extreme, but thousands of reproductions of the works of the painters mentioned have been sold, not only through art stores, but also through department stores and through mail-order merchandising.

GOOD DESIGN

An example of another kind of influence in another area was the series of exhibitions called "Good Design," supervised by Edgar Kaufman, Jr., for the Museum of Modern Art, New York, and the Merchandise Mart in Chicago. Outstanding examples of commercially produced objects, mostly in the field of home furnishings and accessories, were selected by a series of small committees of which Mr. Kaufman was the chairman and continuing member. The objects were displayed in exhibitions designed by such talented men as Charles Eames, Finn Juhl, Paul Rudolph, and Alexander Girard. The exhibitions were widely publicized and well attended and surely affected the design thinking of a number of manufacturers and retailers.

The objects selected for exhibition had to pass the collective judgment of the jury and meet their design criteria. Nearly all the pieces shown were clean-lined, simple in form, and well constructed. Objects with trite decoration and meaningless embellishments just never got shown. It takes time to get such a subtle point across to an audience not used to thinking in these terms; but, in the long run, people do understand what is being said.

Figure 8. *Top:* An advertisement for the Praxis 48 typewriter intended to appeal to the "sharp and tasteful" secretary. Client: Olivetti Underwood Corp., Art Director: Walter Kaprielian. Photographer: James Moore. Agency: Ketchum MacLeod & Grove Inc. *Bottom:* The Praxis 48 was treated as a simple box shape with projecting keyboard. Its compactness creates virtually a new class of typewriters. Client: Olivetti Underwood Corp. Design: Ettore Sottsass Jr. & Hans von Klier.

3

Product Design

The product designer's work functions in an intimate association with people. The objects he designs are used, operated, handled, read, and reacted to by people. The esthetic side of product design is quite as important as the functional side. In fact, it could be said that the term function has two meanings of equal importance. One is related to man's mechanical needs (a drawer that slides easily, a typewriter keyboard that fits one's fingers). His other need is psychological—his need for beauty. So "function" contains two meanings, workability and beauty. For a thing to be completely functional it must satisfy both requirements. It must work; it must be beautiful. Not many objects in our culture satisfy both requirements in any complete sense.

Concerning function: It is an axiom of design that a thing intended to be used by human hands should be shaped to fit the hand, a thing intended to be read must first of all be legible, and a thing intended to be seen must be handsome.

The dual meaning of the term function (workability and beauty) has been echoed by museums across the country. Foremost among these has been the Museum of Modern Art in New York City, which has exhibited as a matter of course the work of industrial designers for many years. This museum also originated the "Good Design" exhibitions of useful objects in conjunction with the Merchandise Mart in Chicago. These exhibitions gave recognition and publicity to fine design in objects for everyday use, generally in connection with home furnishings, furniture, tableware, cooking implements, lamps, and the like. Other museums took up the challenge and well-designed objects became a more familiar part of the museum's educational programs.

The design of a product is nearly always the result of a series of compromises. If the final product is well designed it is because the

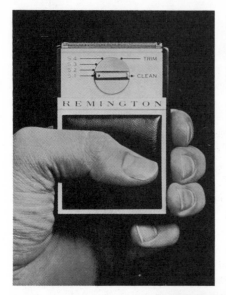 

Figure 9. *Top left:* An electric shaver of unusually straightforward design. Client: Remington Electric Shaver Div., Sperry Rand Corp., Staff Design. *Top right:* The form of this mixer stresses simplicity and ease of cleaning. The dies were made directly from a finished pattern to insure true translation of the subtle transitions from one form to another. Client: Westinghouse Electric Corp. Design: Director Consumer Products, C. F. Graser. *Bottom:* A piece of testing equipment that presents a disarmingly simple face to the world. Controls are held to a minimum, graphics are clear and unaffected, the total impression is one of accuracy and function. Client: Clauser Technology Corp. Design: Don Albinson.

proper choices were made when the alternatives were examined. If it is badly designed the choices may have been badly stated or poorly understood. Cost *vs.* value, reliability *vs.* practicability, size *vs.* weight, elegance *vs.* maintenance: all are questions involving design decisions. The "image" of a company rises or falls on its decisions in these and other areas.

Designers are usually committed to an overall policy of promoting elegance of design, a direct expression of the character and function of the object, and a use of materials and production methods consistent with the final use of the product. While others in decision-making positions are also interested in the appearance of the product, the designer has a much more direct involvement as he is deeply absorbed by this aspect of the total problem. He works with engineers, cost estimators, production and sales experts, management people and specialists from many areas—but of all these he is the most concerned with the total design and its final expression. It is obvious that no one man could be expected to keep up with all the new developments in so many different fields and be expert in all of them. But the designer is expected to be aware of developments in all fields that impinge on his speciality: design. He must know where to go for full information on materials and processes whenever the need arises, and it arises on every job he does. The function of the designer in this regard is often that of a catalyst, bringing together many specialists to jointly arrive at the best solution to a given design problem. In our culture few objects are designed and made by one individual. Products are normally the end result of contributions by a large number of individuals, although one may be said to be responsible for the original idea or concept and may be given credit for the final result.

The first stage in the development of a product is usually that of an engineering-minded man to get something "to work." The design is then often improved as an effort is made to clean up the first try and get the parts organized into a neater package. Next come other refinements, organization of the controls, dials, indicators, handles, and knobs, into better-functioning groups, a general simplification of form and, perhaps, a major change that forces a new form of the object itself.

To use the ubiquitous telephone as an example: from an object standing obtrusively on desk or table, to a lower, fatter object less awkwardly visible, to one smaller and shapelier, to one partially built into the wall, to one completely built-in and for all practical purposes invisible—that is the general trend. What has happened, and is even now still happening, to the telephone has also been happening to many other familiar objects that have for years been important parts of our

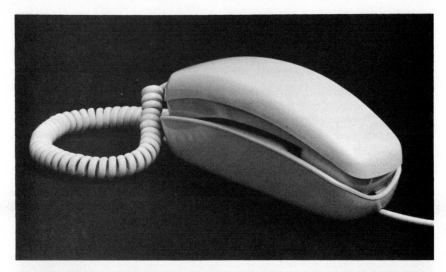

Figure 10. *Above:* The Trimline telephone puts the dial in the handset along with a light. A recall button is provided so the line can be cleared without actually having to "hang up." The design brings the telephone closer to a sculptural concept, long considered an ideal. The Museum of Modern Art included this phone in its Design Collection—the first telephone to be accepted. Client: Bell Telephone Labs. Design Consultant: Henry Dreyfuss. Manufacturer: Western Electric Co. *Opposite:* Action Office furniture resulted from an inquiry into the true activities of office workers: how much time they spent standing, perching, walking, leaning—even reclining. Robert Propst collected data that was passed along to George Nelson who translated it into actual pieces of office equipment. Unusual problems dictate unusual solutions. Client: Herman Miller. Design: George Nelson & Co. Project Director: Ronald Beckman. Photographer: Louis Reems.

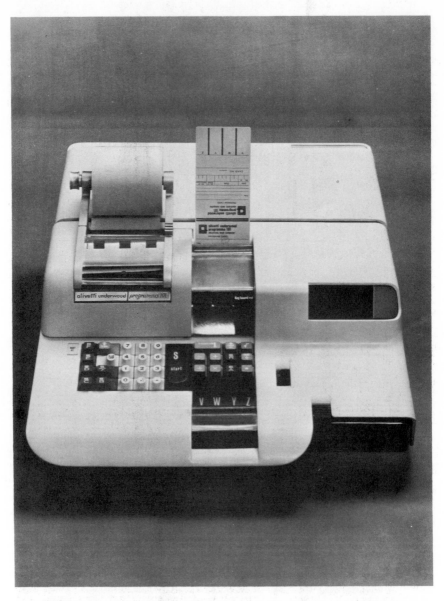

Figure 11. The first desktop computer, the Programma 101, can "write," store and run programs while making logical decisions and is about as large as a standard typewriter. Programs calling for as many as 120 instructions are stored conveniently on magnetic cards (shown inserted). Results are printed out on plain paper tape (left). Client: Olivetti Underwood Co. Design: Staff designers.

environment. Sewing machines, radios, record players, TV sets, typewriters, lighting fixtures, tape recorders, slide and movie projectors, and the like, are all in various stages of change, slowly being absorbed by the house itself, tucked into the structure of the office, concealed in the body of the building.

This leads to a general principle: The best design for an object may well be the elimination of the thing (as a visible object) altogether. There is no particular reason why the form of the telephone, for example, should occupy the designer's waking hours. In the long run it is not the telephone itself that matters but rather that we wish to communicate with someone not within shouting distance—and require some device to accomplish this wish. The less the equipment is an ostentatious part of the scene, the better. In fact, the more it can become an invisible service, the better. The laundress, her washtubs, scrub brushes, and drying lines have been compacted into one or two small pieces of automatic machinery quietly operating when needed in the kitchen, hall, or service area of the house. These pieces of equipment are destined to become more and more compact until they are part of a service core performing cleaning tasks even less obtrusively than before.

Our general needs have increased with the increased number of options offered by our society. The equipment required to fulfill these needs takes a lot of room. As long as it remains visible equipment it certainly ought to be both good looking and functional—but as we refine and develop and miniaturize these things (because, as *things* they have no special significance) we enable a given amount of storage space to do more and more work for us. A wider variety of services can be performed by smaller and smaller pieces of equipment. In our homes and offices, more expensive because of the equipment they contain and therefore smaller than our grandfathers' homes or offices, we live a life of relative luxury. Compare the food, entertainment, cultural activities easily available to the ordinary American with those of nearly any other country. There is a tremendous difference and it is a difference growing even greater in most instances. Our technology is expanding, building, offering us more and more for our time of life.

Along with the tendency to build more and more equipment into our structures goes a tendency to assume a shorter and shorter occupancy on our part. We no longer think of a house as a place to occupy permanently, in which to raise a family that would in its turn continue to live there and raise their young, on and on. We take it for granted that we will sell the house in a matter of a very few years. We expect each new structure (and the equipment it contains)

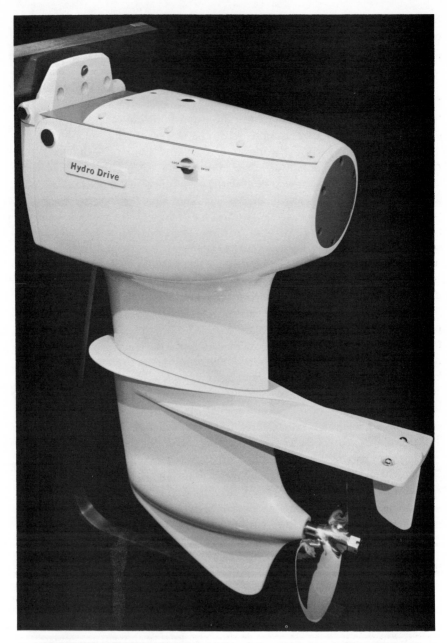

Figure 12. An outboard-mounted drive for an inboard motor. The beautifully sculptured forms are die-cast aluminum making a feature of the recessed bolt heads which certainly could have been unsightly. Client: Hydro Drive Corp. Design: Eliot Noyes and Assoc. (Ernest Bevilacqua & Robert Graf).

to be superior to the one we just vacated. We expect change and usually equate it with improvement. *New* and *better* are synonymous to most people.

Houses as well as cars and other major possessions are often bought with an eye for resale. This changing attitude has another far-reaching effect. With less and less interest in the fact of ownership of things generally—but with a strong interest in their *use*—a rapidly growing part of our society's service industry is that of car leasing and equipment rental. It makes a good deal of sense to rent a large pneumatic drill, a jack hammer, or a cement mixer for a few days rather than to buy things you will not need again for years, if ever. There may also be considerable logic in leasing a vehicle rather than owning it. The growth of condominiums reflects this attitude of minimum involvement along with a desire to obtain equity. Relieve yourself of the drudgery of home ownership but have all the enjoyable aspects through payment of a shared maintenance fee. Relax while a hired gardener mows the grass, swim and sun bathe while someone else does the work you would otherwise have to do.

We are, however, in an interim state in the development of most of the things we currently use. We have not yet dispensed with the things as visible objects while retaining their useful functions. In the meantime we must solve problems of appearance along with other functional aspects of our possessions.

The design of a product often goes through several well-defined stages:

1. Information—the designer collects the facts he needs about the new product, production program of the manufacturer, emphasis to be made as to certain aspects of the program, comparison with other similar products from other firms.
2. Research—who are the people who will use this product, which part of the market is this product aimed for, what are the surroundings in which the product will be used, possible areas of simplification of the product, which production methods are suggested?
3. Design—development of a new idea as to the form of the product; failing this, development of variations of older ideas, following a series of such ideas may lead to a new departure, cooperation and discussion of the problem with people involved in the final production.
4. Decision—recommended solution is shown to management of firm; sales manager is concerned as to salable features; production head is concerned about methods and economy; legal requirements and regulations are the concern of all.

Figure 13. *Top:* The Marbon CRV-2 competition-model car with a two-piece body/chassis of ABS thermoplastic in a clamshell form. Top and bottom halves formed from two sheets of plastic joined at the "belt line" with an all around bumper. Client: Marbon Chemical Div. of Borg Warner Corp. *Bottom:* A tuner and amplifier very neatly packaged for either horizontal or vertical use. The apparent ease with which these units were designed was the result of careful consideration and study on the part of the designer. The simplicity of the construction and jointing is noteworthy. Client: Newtronics Inc. Design: Don Albinson. *Opposite:* The 40-4 chair is shown here as an example of good design for industrial production. Manufacturing methods and materials were as important as appearance and finish. Client: General Fireproofing Co. Design: David Rowland, consultant.

26

DON'T CALL IT AN ADDING MACHINE!

It's not fair.
Not when it multiplies, too. And subtracts. And shows
a credit balance. As well as adding nine columns,
totaling ten—$99,999,999.99. Besides, it prints total,
sub-total and credit balance, with a two-color ribbon.
Ideal for home or office, the CALTEC electric
adding machine is precision crafted of stainless steel
and comes with a one-year warranty on all parts
and 90 days on labor. It weighs only eleven pounds
and it's U.L. approved. Don't call it an adding machine.
Call it a bargain.

Why? Because it's priced at only $129.50

CALTEC

WORLDWIDE OFFICE EQUIPMENT CORPORATION 1246 WEST SECOND STREET, LOS ANGELES, CALIFORNIA 90026

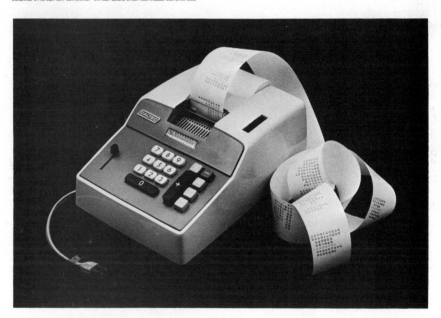

Figure 14. *Top:* An advertisement for a Japanese adding machine that makes good use of the photograph by restraining copy into a reasonable amount and using a bold type face to carry the verbal message. Client: Worldwide Office Equipment Corp. Agency: David Olin Advertising (Gordon Gelfond). Art Director: Stephen Kursh. Photographer: Peter Caine. *Bottom:* A neat packing job for the complex innards of an adding machine. Good contrast between softly rounded edges of the major form with the sharply defined edges of the control panel. Client: Tokyo Electric Co. Design: Staff designers.

5. Calculation—fitting the product into the requirement of the factory and its production standards, care must be exercised to prevent slight alterations of form by those who do not realize the effect on the total design and the possible destruction of the overall concept.
6. Modelmaking—development of a working model to obtain technical information and guidance in production planning. The model may also be used as a sample for advance publicity before production models are available, as for photographic use, and the like.
7. Completion—where it is possible, the designer follows the product through the production line, aiding in solving the immediate problems that always occur in the manufacturing of a new product. He is concerned that the final product realizes the promise of the first concept and is not emasculated along the way.

The first six points just mentioned were suggested by the faculty of the Ulm School of Design, Germany. The last is common practice in the United States. However, each assignment develops along its own lines. No two are alike as no two products really will duplicate each other in all aspects.

Industrial design is a new profession. As such it is also somewhat ambiguous. Definitions of the term *industrial design* will vary according to the background, experience, or training of the person doing the defining. To many people industrial design is simply the shaping of mass-produced objects, giving these things form according to their various functions. To others, the industrial designer is no more than an adjunct of the sales department, restyling the product each year so it looks sufficiently unlike last year's model. To someone else, industrial design is related to the engineering department, a slicking-up of the engineer's solution to a practical problem.

But the industrial designer is neither an engineer, nor an artist, nor a salesman. He combines something of each of those talents and adds a few of his own to create something more than any of these abilities as they stand alone. He knows enough about the engineer's job to discuss with him the best way to solve a given structural problem or to select the most appropriate manufacturing method. He understands sales psychology well enough to be well aware of the buying habits of those who are most likely to purchase the product he is designing. He also knows that past preferences (expressed through purchases of similar goods by the public) are indications only, that the picture could well change if a new or better product were offered to the same buyers.

The industrial designer is aware that the shape, color, texture, finish, and general appearance of a product strongly influence its sale. His

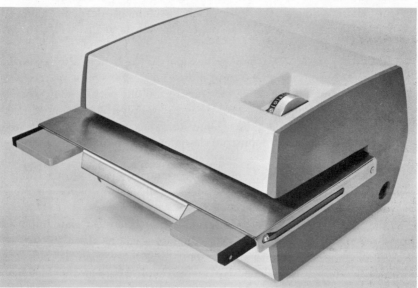

Figure 15. *Top:* The Ski-Lark is a 14-foot molded fiberglass "gull wing" boat with a fold-down windshield, four seats, running lights and steering. It is cleanly designed. Client: Evinrude Motors. Design: Brooks Stevens. *Bottom:* Winner of a Wescon award, this electric imprinter uses a modular approach with constant end pieces and variable lengths. Client: Dashew Business Machines Inc. Design: Stephen G. Hauser. *Opposite:* Passengers in the San Francisco Bay area will travel on fast commuters that are safe, comfortable and convenient. The prototype shown here was approved as the design direction to follow. Trains will be completely computer controlled, close-coupled, with a flexible accordion seal joining them. Client: Bay Area Rapid Transit District. Design: Sundberg-Ferar.

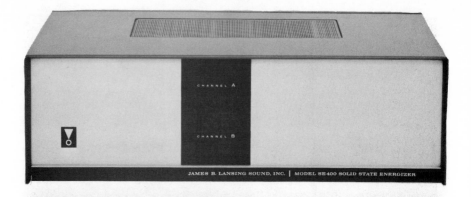

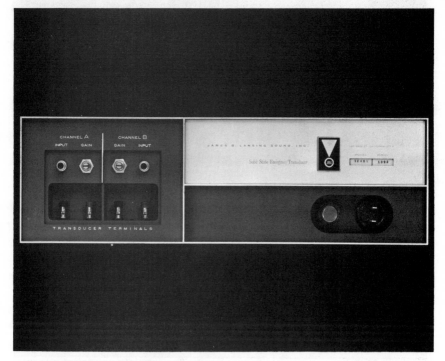

Figure 16. *Above:* Two versions of a new energizer—a built-in unit and a free-standing model. They are crisp, sharp, "unstyled" and one won a Wescon award. Client: James B. Lansing Sound, Inc. Project Director: Lamont J. Seitz. Design: Arnold Wolf. *Opposite top:* An experimental walk-in drive-in vending installation in Kansas City. The advantage of economical 24-hour operation is obvious as is the convenience to travelers who move at all hours. Client: Vendo Co. Design: Staff designers. *Opposite bottom:* Vending machines of modular and related design create a neat line-up for the serving of food and drink. This group is a good indication of the overall improvement in design achieved in recent years by major manufacturers. Client: Vendo Co. Design: Staff designers.

Figure 17. The first American racing machine to defeat all European competitors in endurance contests of 12 hours or more. Clearly a powerful brute of a car, its overall form is sculptured to accommodate ventilation and operational considerations. One of the larger products of concern to a special group of designers, the automobile in all its forms is of major importance within the American economy. Client: Ford GT—Ford Motor Co. Competition program: Shelby American Inc., Los Angeles.

training and experience must prepare him to exercise esthetic judgment constantly in the development of the design of a new product or the redesign of an old one.

The designer looks at everything in the world around him with an eye to its improvement. He asks questions. Can this thing be made in a better way, or a better material, with a better form? Do we really need this thing at all? Could this thing be built into the building (or car or plane or whatever) and thereby become invisible? He looks at an object like a telephone and finds himself developing a series of reactions. The phone occupies desk space that might well be put to better use; it takes two hands to operate while dialing, one hand to hold it while in use. The dialing method is far from convenient and is none too accurate. And, after all, we may not really want an object cluttering up the premises. What we really want is to talk to some-one who is not here at this moment. The less obtrusive the means, the better.

The tendency on the part of the designer might be to make the means of communication less obtrusive while attempting to improve the quality of the communicating device at the same time. Fewer boxes, cases, handles, dials, gadgets. Better quality of sound, easier handling of the few elements you might have to contact, improved convenience, greater value. So sweeping a change might have to be presented to the public in several stages in order to familiarize people with the changes step by step. A program of scheduled improvements laid out well in advance is referred to as *planned* obsolescence—each stage making obsolete the model that preceded it by performing in a way that is really better, by being truly superior.

Another kind of obsolescence is *technological* obsolescence, wherein a significant technical improvement is developed and incorporated in the new model, which then operates in a manner significantly better than the old. This is a general goal to which all designers subscribe through their desire to measurably improve the product while they are giving it its form.

A third kind of obsolescence is *artificial* obsolescence. Here small changes are made, usually in meaningless decorative elements, so that the new model *looks* different from the old but is actually changed in no meaningful way. Whether this chrome ornament goes here—or here—is a matter of little consequence. Through such relatively unimportant annual appearance changes a sizeable number of cars are sold each year, as are several million suits, dresses, shoes—and, now, even re-frigerators.

Figure 18. A multifaceted structure reflects the light from plane to plane in varying degrees of intensity creating a most interesting lighting effect. The light source is concealed by the overlapping of the metal slices that form the structure. Client: Lightolier, Jersey City. Design: Henry Muller, Lightolier design staff.

|4

Home Furnishings

A look at the pages of magazines in which home furnishings are shown and advertised could well lead one to the conclusion that there is a strange, bewildering, frustrating situation now existing in this area of human activity. Furniture, lamps, clocks, ash trays, dishes, tableware, TV sets, record players, and radios not only are available in great abundance; they are also available in a stupefying variety of "styles." Roman epic opulence vies with frantic French decorativism; immovable Mexican solidity is exhibited next to blond Scandinavian simplicity; Colonial American provincialism and Mediterranean massiveness sit cheek by jowl. Good, bad, and indifferent, all are available to all. The peculiar thing is that we are talking about fake effects rather than attempts to solve real problems for living in an age of electronics, computers, and space exploration.

Looking at the average American home one would never know this was the end of the twentieth century, unless one looked behind the face of the wall clock, with its rough whittled numbers and wood mixing spoon hands, to discover the mechanism was such that it will run for a year on two little flashlight batteries. Inside the heavily carved wood cabinet with its copies of sixteenth century Moorish hinges is an intricate and marvelous piece of equipment that can reproduce all manner of sounds, including those higher and lower than the human ear can register, with eight speakers conveying all the quality of the original musical performance. The recording played through this equipment may be of the Philadelphia Symphony Orchestra. More likely it will be by groups such as the esoteric Carl Click and his Clacques, The Soul Survivors, the current rage Piggy and the Squealers, or that charming pair of folk singers, Sodom and Gomorrah.

Despite the nature of the sounds that emanate from the cabinet, the miracle of the mechanism inside remains. The cabinet may be

Figure 19. *Above:* This imaginatively designed flatware was created for SAS Airlines' use. These shapely eating tools are used in the tourist-class accommodations and are far more attractive than the conventional silver service used by the first-class passengers. Economy has unexpected rewards. Client: SAS Airlines. Design: Sigurd Persson. *Opposite top:* Part of a collection of furniture designed for use in homes and offices. Client: Herman Miller Co. Design: George Nelson. Photo: Ezra Stoller. *Opposite bottom:* Furniture intended for both indoor and outdoor use. Of vinyl material stretched between cast-aluminum side pieces. Excellent ability to resist wear and weather, along with sinuous form, makes this furniture both practical and beautiful. Client: Herman Miller Co. Design: Charles Eames.

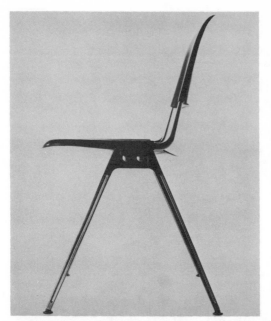

Figure 20. *Top:* Chair designed for stacking and for fitting into groups of chairs plus tables. Aluminum frames and injection molded textured plastic shell. Very lightweight—9 lbs. per chair. Client: Knoll Associates. Design: Don Albinson. *Bottom:* Classic in its elegant restraint and subtle in its form, this china makes its point through understatement and a reliance on the quality of the material used. Note the shape of the handle and the flair of the lip of the cup. Client: Minton Inc. Design: Staff designers.

an anachronism, a strange choice at violent odds with the marvels it contains. Why should the cabinet *not* be consistent with its contents? Why should the exterior and interior *not* be one and the same in concept, direction, and execution? Why should anyone even consider a different course?

The principles of design followed by those who are the leaders in all fields of design include simplicity, appropriate form, function, and overall economy. Imitation, fraudulent styles and mannerisms have nothing to do with good design—and never have had. And if logic were the only criterion, that would be all that need be said.

People are, however, not often very logical. They respond to dreams, fantasies, emotional appeals, and prejudices every bit as much as to logic and objectivity. And that is where the "style" approach gets its strength. How else explain such an odd phenomenon?

Styles are a kind of three-dimensional make-believe, an attempt to borrow elegance, prestige, and status from people (usually deceased) in other countries and from other centuries. We steal and adopt their decorative motifs, using them as a superficial wrapping to surround our technology.

It is no accident that the best examples of modern furniture were created by architects like Mies van der Rohe, Le Corbusier, Eero Saarinen, Charles Eames, Alvar Aalto, Marcel Breuer. Their training included exposure to principles based on a search for functional forms and honest structure. In the early days of modern architecture there was no furniture available that could match the directness of the new buildings. The architect was forced to design chairs and tables as well as the buildings in order to have a degree of consistency in the entire job. No one else apparently knew how.

Since that beginning the best furniture usually followed the same pattern. Structural parts were often exposed and, therefore, had to be acceptably handsome and finished as much as any other part. The major problem in design is at the point where two materials come together—the connection. No matter how well all other elements are handled the solution stands or falls on the connections. This is true in architecture, furniture, or any other three-dimensional object.

A designer approaches the design of a chair, for example, by giving serious consideration to the manner in which people sit, their general measurements, weight, changes of position, degree of softness or firmness desirable for the kind of sitting they are doing (eating dinner, studying, lounging with a drink nearby, in idle conversation, waiting to have a tooth pulled), the probable environment in which the chair will be used, the type of upholstery most logical for such a use (fabric, vinyl, leather), and many, many other similar factors. Please

Figure 21. *Above:* Much of today's storage is modular and rear-rangeable. Equipment may be located at any height, elements may be added or removed at will, flexibility is assured by the system used. The chair is by Charles Eames for the same manufacturer. Client: Herman Miller Co. Design: George Nelson. *Opposite top:* A stainless steel design called "Odin" in which the shape of the knives recalls that of Viking oars. Client: Dansk. Design: Jens H. Quistgaard. *Opposite bottom:* Heat-forged stainless steel with black nylon handles. A restrained and elegant design offering a contrast of materials and finishes. Client: Dansk. Design: Jens H. Quistgaard.

43

Figure 22. *Top left:* This decanter and glasses are part of a complete range of glassware made possible through the use of new techniques in glassmaking. Higher production resulted in no loss of esthetic quality. Client: Caithness Glass Ltd., Scotland. Design: Domnhall OBrein. *Top right:* A lamp of almost irreducible simplicity, part of a line that has won many awards for outstanding design. Selected by the U.S. Dept. of Commerce for display in Yugoslavia and Iraq as examples of good design from America. Chosen by "Industrial Design" magazine as best lamps of the year. (See also the first illustration in this book.) Client: Design Line, Inc. Design: Bill Curry. *Bottom:* Bearing an unconditional guarantee against damage due to thermal shock, these dishes are suitable for use in the freezer, refrigerator, broiler, or on the burner—as well as for serving at the table. These pieces are intended as high-style food preparation and serving utensils with their decoration restricted to the material of which they are made. Client: Corning Glass Works. Design: Sam Mann consultant; Ronald G. De Puy.

note: these are all functional considerations. The word "style" does not arise as the designer is attempting to create a new chair, not re-create someone else's solution to another problem from another culture. The designer is interested in his own time and its problems—as were Chippendale and Hepplewhite in their time. The simple fact is, their time and our time are not at all the same. The whole world has changed so as to be almost unrecognizable to our ancestors.

To mention only material changes, think what capable men of two hundred years ago could have done if they had had aluminum, magnesium, vinyl, fiberglass, molded plywood, laminates. While it is probably idle to speculate on such fancies the point remains; Chippendale did the best he could for the people of his culture. He considered the way in which they would use his furniture, their habits, clothing, customs, and needs. He created furniture suited to their pattern of living. He was a modern designer of his day and should be considered such.

In addition to differences in available materials, our time is unlike our forefathers' in other ways as well. There is a discipline necessary to the designer who is thinking in terms of the machine. Mass production calls for infinite care in planning and preparation. Simplification of details, use of materials that lend themselves to production techniques, finishes and coatings that can be automatically applied, and possible nesting of parts for economical shipping are all considerations of importance to the designer. Along with these problems comes a certain reward—many processes that would be uneconomical in the production of a few units become quite feasible in quantities of a thousand or more. And the end result can be a piece of high quality furniture at a most reasonable price. Good design certainly does not cost more than poor design. In the long run it costs far less.

PROJECTIONS

Some of the most exciting ideas in furniture design lie in the direction of the elimination of furniture, at least as a visible thing. One line of thought has been proposed by William Katavolos. Chemical materials have been developed that, when suitably treated, expand to great size, catalize, and become rigid. It should soon be possible to build into these chemicals preferred patterns of behavior in order to produce structural forms of our own choosing. This could make it possible to use small quantities of powder and make them expand into forms such as hollow spheres and tubes large enough for us to inhabit.

The floor might be a crystalline cellular grid into which a variety of disposable pods could be plugged. One type of pod could contain

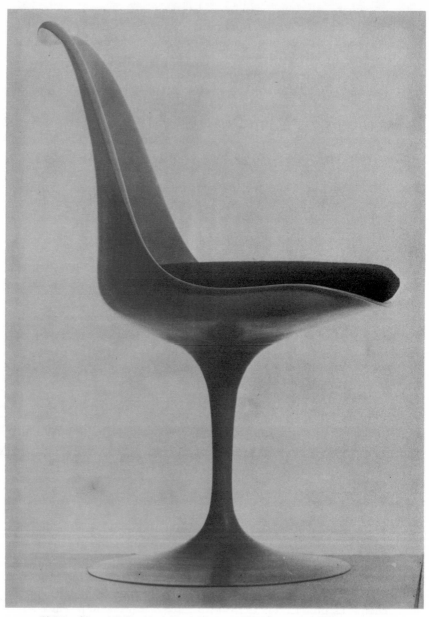

Figure 23. *Above:* A side chair in fiberglass and spun aluminum. An attempt to minimize the "leggy" look results in a chair like a wineglass on its slender stem. Client: Knoll Associates. Design: Eero Saarinen. *Opposite top left:* The 40-4 is so-called because 40 chairs stack only 4 feet high. Client: General Fireproofing Co. Design: David Rowland. *Opposite top right:* The designer obviously cared about handles fitting hands. Slender, graceful, elegant, practical, easy to

clean, with a long useful life—these implements are design at its best. Client: Lauffer. Design: Don Wallance. *Directly above:* This design was created for hard use in restaurants, hotels, hospitals, colleges, and country clubs. The shapes are strong but simple. Client: Shenango China, Inc. Design: W. Craig McBurney.

Figure 24. Beautifully shaped porcelain produced as companion pieces to the world-famous Arzberg porcelain, this brand has received its share of recognition and awards. Client: Fairwood China, Bavaria. Design: Heinrich Loeffelhardt, Germany.

a "chair," which, through chemical action, could rise through pressure to receive the sitter, softly descend to a more comfortable height and position, even bring him warmth or coolness, vibration or flex—even stereophonic sound.

Such furniture has the final advantage of disappearing back into the floor when no longer needed. Sound rather far-out? So was putting a man on the moon just a few years ago, or condensing a one-hundred-piece orchestra into a small reel of plastic tape.

Even Charles Eames, perhaps the most famous furniture designer of our time, invited once to participate in a discussion concerned with the design and furnishing of a new school (intended to be the most up-to-date anywhere) mildly suggested the possible elimination of most of the regular school furniture through manipulation of the floor and wall surfaces to permit them to do much of the work normally done by desks and chairs. The other participants in the discussion were not quite ready for this concept, so very little was done about it. A good idea requires a receptive audience.

Figure 25. The Chicago showroom of a well-known New York manufacturer of top quality furniture and accessories. The arrangement suggests spaciousness and an elegant restraint that matches the quality of the individual pieces. Client: Laverne International. Design: Erwine and Estelle Laverne.

5

Interiors

The term *interior design* covers a very broad spectrum of work—from the classic, elegant, restrained "Mies van der Rohe" interior to the chi-chi, frou-frou decor a la Madame Pompadour. Those who follow the latter direction express concern over such monumental problems as "what goes with what" in the game of musical chairs represented by the many many styles from which one may choose. These decorators "express the personality of the client" through a selection from, let us say, Louis XXIX (or any appropriate number), blithely disregarding the fact that Louis' furniture might have been quite appropriate for him—but that was in another time, another place, and for another way of life. What a peculiar client it must be whose personality and needs fit best into another century, another country, another culture —and evidently do not fit at all into this century, this country, this culture!

You may change the game from Louis XXIX to any other style. The principle remains the same. People are still trying to borrow culture, refinement, and status by a purchase at the local furniture store. After all, this method is so much easier on the customer. He does not now have to read books, study history, develop his understanding through exposure to a knowledge of, and a taste for, worthwhile things. He need not earn his status—only buy the right *fayteuil* (whatever that is). The main difficulty with this method is its remarkably short life, as the "right" style keeps changing. This season it is Immobile Mexican with handcrafted iron hinges, next it is Cathedral Gothic with a twelfth century influence and bas-relief saints carved into the backs of the chairs. Next may be Palatial Peruvian with llama-hide upholstery for the chairs and a dandy hand-woven cover for the TV set with alpaca tail tassels of course. And what comes next is anybody's guess.

Figure 26. The reception area of the architectural firm of Welton Becket and Associates, Los Angeles, makes a statement on the nature of space and materials and suggests the character of the work done by this firm. Across the pool/court is a glass-walled board room for staff meetings and conferences with clients. Client: Welton Becket and Associates. Design: Staff designers.

Isn't this an aimless way to stagger into the future—by dredging up everybody else's past, piecemeal or entire?

By way of contrast to the foregoing, the existence of objects fitted to our way of life depended on an investigation into the function of these objects and a rejection of the very idea of stylistic imitation. Creative and serious individuals began early in this century looking into the real potentials of materials and manufacturing processes with a view to using them to express the essence of our own time in a straightforward and appropriate manner. The position of these people was, essentially, a moral one, a matter of honesty. No borrowing of Louis XXIX (or anyone else's) decorative mannerisms, as these had absolutely nothing to do with the problems of the twentieth century. The fakery of manufacturing mass-produced ornamentation for "authentic antique replicas" was disavowed. The aim was for good design in everything from a spoon to a house, everyday objects of real esthetic worth for everybody who wanted them.

Some fifty or sixty years later it seems clear the battle has, in a real sense, been won, Louis XXIX notwithstanding. Those who tried to introduce a note of sanity into the proceedings have, within limits, succeeded. Modern furniture (if we may use that term to denote well-designed furniture) exists in a broad array of types, prices, and levels of quality. There are some quite expensive pieces of furniture that are examples of fine materials and craftsmanship, but there are also thousands of relatively inexpensive pieces that have excellent form and are quite durable as well. Over a million chairs produced from the designs of just one man, Charles Eames, are in use at this moment to point to one, admittedly unusual, example.

Office interiors are changing from places where papers are shuffled around to places where information is handled, often in automated ways. Thousands of bits of data need to be sorted and cross-filed, indexed and available, yet cleared away and out of sight when not wanted. Many designers are now thinking in terms of housing the necessary equipment in elegant unobtrusive cabinets or desks or behind simple wall panels.

This kind of working space could well have all the warmth, elegance, and quality of any well-designed living room or study. Although our lives (business lives especially) are filled with pieces of paper (reports, memos, notes, agenda, references, lists), these things are even now in the process of becoming magnetic impulses on a reel of tape, available when needed but in a most condensed form meanwhile.

The general furnishings for such a work area should be created with an eye toward developing an appropriate psychological climate as well as providing the facilities with which to do business in today's

Figure 27. *Top:* A stairwell at the center of a large store with lightly suspended figures hovering overhead. The spacious effect is augmented by the varying levels of illumination. Design: Welton Becket and Associates. *Bottom:* A children's department in a large store. The light touch is established in the amusing sign and carries through in the wood slat park bench seats. Design: Welton Becket and Associates.

sophisticated world. Executives have come a long way from the old golden-oak roll-top desk against the wall, through a monumental desk decorated with mementos (but never with work), to no desk at all, perhaps. If there is such a thing as a desk, its design surely grew from a detailed study of the function it was to perform. Some of the new Herman Miller office pieces are a sharp departure from anything seen even in the recent past owing to an analysis of what the occupant of the office actually did during his workday. How much time did he spend sitting at a desk, standing, walking? How could the furniture and equipment he needed be made more appropriate for the things he actually did rather than conform to some decorator's conception of how an office ought to look?

Every significant change in design, whether it be in office interiors or showrooms, retail outlets, lobbies, motel rooms, and the like, has grown from an analysis of function. The better the problem was stated and the more direct the study, the better the possible solution. Good solutions to problems do not come as the result of someone's whim or "flair for color" or a decorator's feeling that Barnyard Baroque is just the thing for the office of a cereal company president. Good solutions come from a clearer and clearer understanding of the real nature of the problem coupled with creative imagination and trained ability.

Ideas must be accurately communicated to those who are to execute them. The designer must be able to make the drawings, sketches, renderings, and models that will show, visually, his intent. He must be capable of writing specifications that spell out the quality, size, brand, and color required to make the final interior live up to the original concept. Interior design has had to live down the poor reputation it garnered as the inevitable result of a large number of "little old ladies" of both sexes and many ages "doing" interiors without the benefit of training, education, or experience. Their stock in trade was often a pack-rat knowledge of the location and price of odd accessories, pieces of furniture, and strange lighting fixtures. Their method was often a vague verbal description accompanied by much hand waving. "The bibelot will look just marvelous over here and the drapes will be tied back with a brass chain with a simple massive escutcheon that will be repeated in the frame of the mirror on this persimmon wall with an original Sans-sens on the pink wall over there, etc., etc." Some tradesmen loved this kind of job, as nothing was ever really clear enough to pin down responsibility or quality and costs had a way of mounting all along the way. Every change—and there would be lots of them—upped the cost again.

Figure 28. The central hall of this school in Greeley, Colorado, has been depressed into a series of circular step/seats that are used as another classroom. Story time can certainly be an enjoyable experience in such a setting. Client: School District 6, Greeley, Colorado. Design: John Shaver, Salinas, Kansas.

Good workmen, however, would much rather know where they stand, would rather be proud of the job they do when it is done. They prefer to work with competent designers who speak their language and understand their problems.

Proper training for interior design includes the development of skill in drawing and rendering; ability to speak the language of the architect and builder; ability to produce accurate floor plans, sections, elevations, and details required for the work; knowledge of lighting, acoustics, traffic patterns, and buying habits; sources of well-designed furniture and accessories; knowledge of principles of form, color, texture, space, line, and their application to problems in interior space design. Experience in the business of business is also essential. Record-keeping, organizing one's own work load, working for a profit, understanding billing, taxes, and overhead are all a part of the operation of a successful business regardless of the talent, taste, or personality of the designer.

There are a great many schools and colleges in the United States with interior design classes listed in their catalogs. Many of these appear to be oriented toward answering the young housewife's question of what style goes with what. Only a small handful of schools seriously attempt the difficult task of graduating professional interior designers who are fully qualified to enter the profession. Typically, these few schools use as instructors qualified professional interior designers who have achieved a certain status within their field, men and women who run their own offices four days a week, teaching the fifth day. They bring into the classroom experience that is not only extensive but also current. The problems they present to their students usually follow present practice so far as techniques and methods are concerned. But, along with the development of technical skills, there goes a commitment to pursue the practical facts of the business world.

The differences between the interior designer and the decorator are due partly to differences in training and partly to differences in interest. The designer thinks much as an architect or industrial designer thinks, as a creative person concerned with solving problems of function as well as esthetics. He hopes to create an environment conducive to better living in a complete sense, making for greater ease in use, fewer problems in care and maintenance, greater beauty through more intelligent selection and arrangement of design elements (furniture pieces, carpeting texture, color, and lighting).

The decorator, by contrast, is typically superficial in his work. His approach is often purely an ornamental one, collecting and placing objects into an interior, objects used less for their intrinsic esthetic worth than for their shock or conversational value.

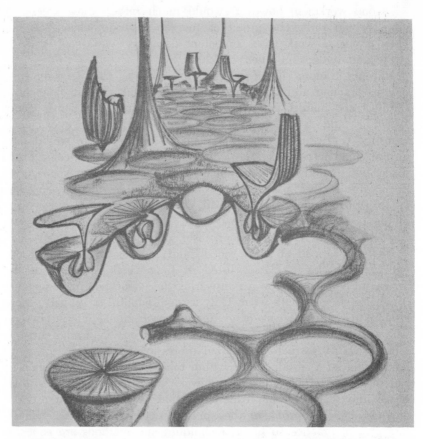

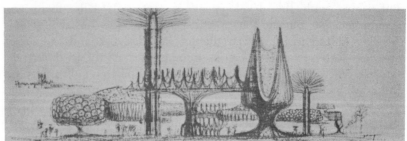

Figure 29. *Above and opposite:* Both house and furnishing are created through chemical action. The character of the desired form would be built into the basic powder followed by chemical expansion into the proper size. The honeycomb floor would contain openings into which could be plugged suitable pods, some of which could act as chairs, others as tables, and so on. On demand, a chair pod would erect itself from the "floor," provide chemical warmth or coolness, flex or vibration, etc. Design concept: William Katavolos.

The design of commercial interiors has developed in recent years almost into a formula. For example, a reception area: the components are several Mies "Barcelona" chairs, a glass-topped coffee table or two, a thick area rug, plaster walls painted off-white, one wall of wood in a dark natural finish, a modern painting and/or sculpture. Arrange according to the available space and necessary traffic patterns, mix with one or two small spots of strong color, add a dash of space, stir in a dollop of texture and presto—a very passable interior is born. Not a great interior, perhaps, but one that possesses most of the earmarks of an acceptable level of taste.

It might, at first glance, seem regrettable that the whole thing is, apparently, so easy. Of course it is not that easy at all. However, it might not be regrettable even if it were easy. Better to have a great many rather good (clean, uncluttered, simple) interiors that utilize the best furniture our time has to offer rather than accept a lower level of performance in the name of what?—individuality (whose?), uniqueness, self-expression (the decorators?), or mere novelty?

The number of manufacturers producing outstanding pieces is quite limited. Once you have named Herman Miller and Knoll Associates you have mentioned the two firms that are known worldwide for marketing the very best in furniture today. There are others of course: Laverne, Dux, Directional, Lunning, Jens Risom, JG, Stendig, and others. Their products, too, are well designed, clean, modern, intended for use in a civilized place by civilized people. There is a wide range of choices, in both character and price, available.

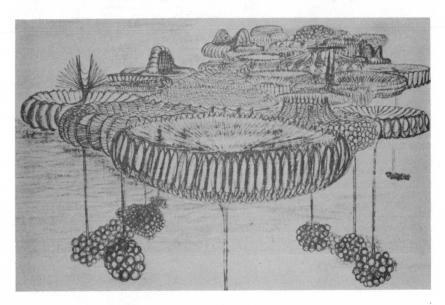

What's the ugliest part of your body?

You just said, "my feet", didn't you?

That's typical.

Most women feel their feet are the least attractive part of their body.

Up until now all a woman could do was hide them.

But now there's something you can do to make them pretty.

Not just passable. Pretty.

Now there's a product named, appropriately enough, Pretty Feet.

Pretty Feet is a pleasant roll-off lotion.

Pour a little on your fingers every day of the week and rub it into your feet.

Then see the rough, dead skin roll right off.

Soon you'll have beautiful feet that can wear open sandals...lovely feet that won't hide in the sand at the beach...smooth feet that won't run stockings...soft feet that will be as sexy as the rest of you.

If you're genuinely interested in making the ugliest part of your body pretty, we'll be happy to start you off with a free sample bottle of Pretty Feet.

Just write to Pretty Feet, Dept. G2, Chemway Corp., Fairfield Road, Wayne, New Jersey.

Figure 30. Rather than give the whole show away by showing only feet and a package of the product in their advertisement, a series was developed that attractively called attention to feet in a circuitous manner. The challenging headline captures the reader's attention, the excellent photograph assures him the copy will be worth reading and the text itself is intelligently organized and well stated. Client: Pretty Feet, Chemway Corp. Agency: Delenanty Kurnit & Geller, Inc. Art Director: Peter Hirsch. Copywriter: Jerry Della Femina. Photographer: William Helburn.

60

6

Advertising Design

The thing called "advertising" is a vast disjointed entity of which only a part is visible at any one time. The American way of life is unimaginable without advertising, in fact, impossible without it. At a graduation ceremony at The Art Center College of Design recently, this point was brought home with humor and clarity by the principal speaker, Wayne Tiss. Mr. Tiss was formerly Vice President of the advertising firm of Batten, Barton, Durstine and Osborn and is still a special consultant to that firm. He spoke from forty years of significant top-level experience in the field and the story he told both amused and instructed his audience. Because of its immediacy, part of his story, entitled "The Day Advertising Stopped," follows:

Senator Ambrose Scraggs—a man of great wrath—arose in the Senate on June 10 and made a long speech against advertising. He let the fur fly. He said that advertising is an economic waste, that it increased the cost of goods to the consumer, that it was often misleading—if not actually deceitful, that it made people buy a lot of things they didn't need, that it appealed to the lowest motives in human beings, that it was often offensive to good taste and that, anyway, it was just a way of charging large business expenses on corporate tax returns—and that the government was being cheated of its rightful income thereby.

The reaction to this speech was amazing. Tired advertising men read it and their universal reaction was, "Oh, what the ——." They suddenly began to think of what they had been promising themselves all these years. One by one at first, then dozens, then hundreds and then by thousands—all 50,000 men in advertising quit and retired. They bought their chicken farms. They snapped up their fishing boats. They started their mail order businesses. There wasn't a soul left in advertising. And so, one day in June advertising stopped.

What happened then is very interesting. Letters and telegrams of congratulations poured in on Senator Scraggs. "I can enjoy my favorite television show now without all those terrible commercials," said one housewife. An econo-

61

Figure 31. *Above:* One fine example of many by famed artist Ben Shahn, this used as a cover illustration for a major CBS-TV script. Other illustrations were used throughout the script. Client: Columbia Broadcasting System. Art Director: William Golden. Artist: Ben Shahn. *Right:* Without a doubt the strongest and most universally recognized symbol used in television broadcasting. Appearing in many variations, the "eye" has so completely dominated the scene that no one else seems able to use an eye as a symbol in competition. Client: Columbia Broadcasting System. Design: William Golden.

mist predicted that prices would come down now that they didn't have to include the fat costs of advertising. For one glorious day Senator Scraggs basked in almost universal praise. And then—

The next day the television and radio networks suspended operations and announced that they would not resume unless the government advanced them an operating fund of 100 million dollars. This would keep them going only a short while. They would need nearly half a *billion* dollars a year to operate without advertising. The New York Times, which had been selling for 5¢, raised its price to 25¢ per copy and solemnly predicted that if circulation fell off as expected they would have to raise the price to 50¢. Time Magazine advanced its price from 25¢ to a dollar a copy, and cut its size in half. All 2,617 trade and professional journals suspended publication.

Emergency management sessions were held in every industry across the country, and the curt conclusions they arrived at snapped like bullets across the land. "The day of the supermarket," said an A & P release, "is over unless advertising is resumed. Self-service is possible only when customers are pre-sold by advertising."

The automobile industry cancelled orders for new tools and dies. "We cannot bring out new models," said a General Motors release, "without the power to publicize them in the entire car-buying market. If the situation continues, the era of mass production of automobiles, as we have known it, is past. The business will return to the situation of 40 years ago when there were over 800 car manufacturers and the average man could not afford one."

Department stores were able to read the future with accuracy because they had had brief experience with newspaper strikes when their regular advertising schedules were interrupted. They immediately cancelled buying orders and laid off an average of 25% of their retail sales staff.

Senator Scraggs, who had been a hero for one short day, now became the target for complaints such as he had never dreamed. A committee of morticians called on him and pointed out that when death notice advertising was halted, attendance at funerals fell off. Painters and electricians who worked on outdoor signs picketed the capitol. Inventors protested that they would be unable to find a market for their new engineering marvels.

The noise of protest steadily mounted in volume as more and more businesses realized the stunning new development that would hobble their work. The White House was ringed with reporters who wanted to know what the government was going to do. Would the U. S. start its own Federal advertising service to promote the goods and services of American industry to itself? Would the government subsidize the trade and professional journals to keep trade informed? Was this socialism? What were they going to do?

The White House said "No comment," and sent for Senator Scraggs. He stayed there for almost 24 hours—one of the longest meetings on record. The next day he rose in the U. S. Senate and delivered the most important speech in his career. I will quote briefly from it:

"I had no idea," said Senator Scraggs, "that advertising men were so sensitive. I have said much worse things about my political opponents and they never retire. I now say this to my friends in the advertising business—please

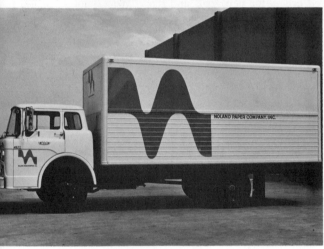

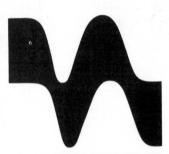

NOLAND PAPER COMPANY, INC.

Figure 32. *Above:* Like the end of a roll of paper unwinding, this symbol works equally well on the letterhead, the face of a building, or the side of a truck. Based on a script letter N, the symbol is most effective in all its varied uses. Client: Noland Paper Co. Design: Ray Engle and Associates, Los Angeles. *Opposite:* A recent change of administration led to a whole new image for Braniff Airlines. This change was accomplished through the use of color, graphic design, new interiors in booking and waiting areas, a new logotype, redesigned tickets, etc., all designed by Alexander Girard. New hairstyles and uniforms were created by Emilio Pucci. The reversible coats, pastel colored boots, removable and interchangeable jackets, wrap-around skirts, culottes and blouses are in a wild variety of colors: fuschia, lilac, turquoise, green and yellow. A plastic bubble headgear protects the hairdo in rainy weather. Please note most of the changes are visual ones and are those most noticeable by the traveling public. Client: Braniff International. Interior and Graphic Design: Alexander Girard. Clothing and Coiffures: Emilio Pucci.

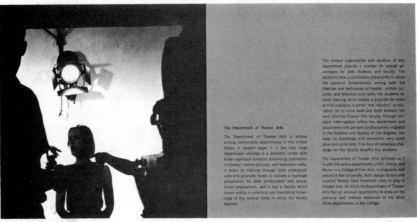

Figure 33. *Top:* Many paper manufacturers sell their products through well-designed brochures, booklets, and mailing pieces aimed at those who design advertising and specify the paper stock to be used by the printer. This spread is from such a booklet, one devoted to the idea of the envelope and the possibilities inherent in its simple structure. Client: Champion Papers Inc. Concept: Needham Louis and Brorby Inc. Design: Tom Kamifuji. *Bottom:* A spread from a brochure on the College of Fine Arts, UCLA. Appropriately dramatic photography and controlled use of type make for an effective layout. Client: University of California at Los Angeles. Design: Robert Heinecken.

come back. We need you. Get out of this lousy chicken farm business, sell your rocky fishing boats, forget your mail order businesses. Do what is necessary, but get back to your desks because I'm about to tell the American people some of the things I've learned about advertising in the last 24 hours." The rest of Senator Scraggs' speech I will paraphrase.

The point of this story is that advertising is the heart muscle of American communication in this country—television, radio, magazines, newspapers. Perhaps this isn't the best way, but it is the way our country is built. We have far and away the finest communications this world has ever seen. The price that America pays for this communication network is the privilege of allowing businessmen to sell their wares by way of this communication system.

As Dr. John Dollard of Yale University puts it, "Advertising is the voice of the seller in a free market . . . advertising can be controlled in any way we want as speech and the press are controlled by law and public taste; but it cannot be eliminated without eliminating, at the same time, the present form of our society."

TRADEMARKS

Many designers of packaging, advertising, and products have made excursions into the field of the design of the corporate symbol. These design fields overlap so much that it is perfectly natural that this be the case. Each field is deeply concerned with design in many phases—and the design (or redesign) of a company's trademark is often the first visible step in a complete program of visual modernization. From the symbol to letterheads to products to office interiors to the buildings themselves, the drive and enthusiasm generated in one area may carry over into others. Because all these are so closely related it is proper that all facets of a company's image be periodically re-examined and updated.

The symbol needs to sum up the essence of the company. It must be a kind of shorthand statement of the goals, aspirations and accomplishments of the firm—and that is asking a lot of a little mark. In today's market and in line with today's thinking the trademark ought to be naturally and closely associated with the activities of the company for which it stands. Many of the older trademarks no longer function in this manner. Many are "dated" to the point of having no real meaning to the younger generation that forms such a large part of today's market.

Most trademarks fail to live up to a high standard of performance. Most are trite, dated, or contrived in form. Some very handsome symbols suggest absolutely nothing of the character of the business they were intended to epitomize. The designer can fall prey to admiration for his own work. The new symbol is so clever, so shapely, so strong

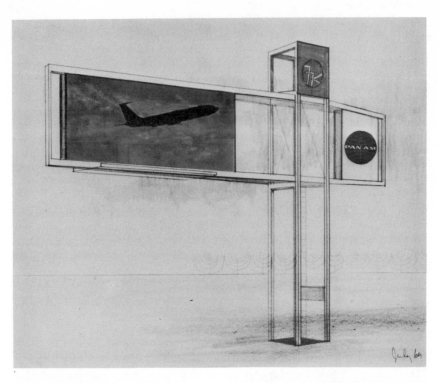

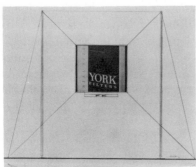

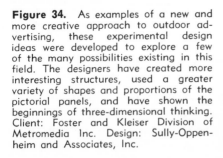

Figure 34. As examples of a new and more creative approach to outdoor advertising, these experimental design ideas were developed to explore a few of the many possibilities existing in this field. The designers have created more interesting structures, used a greater variety of shapes and proportions of the pictorial panels, and have shown the beginnings of three-dimensional thinking. Client: Foster and Kleiser Division of Metromedia Inc. Design: Sully-Oppenheim and Associates, Inc.

that he does not see that it may also be irrelevant. The good designer, however, is not satisfied to develop one or two variations of one idea but works out literally dozens of designs in an attempt to best fulfill the requirements of the problem. He ruthlessly discards appealing designs that fail in some way to solve the real requirements, keeping only the ones that perform properly. These in turn are examined until one design appears to solve the problem best. This design may be examined by all levels of the company's administration before it is accepted and put into use.

OUTDOOR ADVERTISING

Most outdoor advertising has taken the form of a large flat two-dimensional surface on which pictures and lettering are applied. If the graphic design itself is interesting, we tend to ignore the banality of the structure supporting it. If the message is uninspired, we mutter to ourselves something to the effect that those billboards ought to be removed.

In heavily built-up city areas signs, displays, and billboards now appear to be natural elements of the scene, although one could wish for a more imaginative presentation of the advertising. Oddly enough, everyone would miss the signs that give Times Square a kind of excitement at night if those lighted signs were actually removed. The signs are part of the environment and could be legitimate sources of more than trivial, erotic, or banal emotional reactions, if the talents of more creative designers were focused on the problem. The quaint symbolic signs (boots, eyeglasses, roosters) of one area of Copenhagen may not be the right approach for an American metropolis, but neither is the badly painted, quite ugly wall sign covering the width of the fascia of each of the stores in the block nor the stick-out (stuck on) signs with a liberal sprinkling of neon or burned-out light bulbs for "artistic effect." Many architects shudder at the sight of their beautiful structures belatedly surmounted by gross superstructures carrying badly proportioned lettering in blatant colors. Everything the building stood for has been contradicted by the signs added later as a peculiar kind of afterthought. Design responsibility certainly should extend to the entire structure, including all visual elements and especially those as overwhelming in their effect as signs and lettering.

Along every business street, signs and billboards are to be found in great abundance. They perform a necessary function—and with better design would also perform that function better. They display and aid in the acceptance of new products and new ideas. They disseminate information of many kinds. They are often ugly. They need not be.

Figure 35. *Above:* A symbol for "balanced power"—the use of both gas and electricity. The gas flame and the electric plug tell the story. Client: Southern California Gas Co. Design: Jerome Gould Associates, Inc. *Right:* This TV commercial takes advantage of the nature of the medium in its humorous good spirits. Client: Laura Scudder. Agency: Doyle Dane Bernbach. Art Director: Si Lam. *Opposite top:* A poster to increase library use. Client: British Broadcasting Corp. Design: Crosby/Fletcher/Forbes/Gill. *Opposite center:* Offbeat mailing piece of real wood chips aimed at potential customers of the client's firebrick materials. Client: Kaiser Refractory. Agency: Foote Cone and Belding. Art Director: Dave Sanchez. Design: Gollin and Bright. Photographer: Roger Marshutz. *Opposite bottom:* A symbol for a utility company that represents an electric plug. Now used on all forms, signs, trucks, and others. Client: Southern California Edison Co. Design: Jerome Gould Associates, Inc.

THIS COMMERCIAL
HAS BEEN TEMPORARILY
INTERRUPTED DUE TO THE
NOISE OF THE PRODUCT

70

Use your leisure creatively

Do-it-yourself is not the exclusive province of the escapist or the impoverished. BBC broadcasts in sound and television to those who do it themselves prove by the size of their audiences that there is a desire in most of us to exploit our latent talents, however content we may be with the means by which we make our living. In their spare time, engine drivers become electricians, and doctors sculptors; housewives build boats, and typists telescopes. The books here on display will help you to pursue subjects which attract your interest and to give a professional touch to your activities. Subjects range from household repairs to the arts, and the librarian has many more books that he will be pleased to discuss with you. Enquire, too, about leisure classes which your local authority may be running. Make the most of your talents and your leisure.

(BBC) Broadcasts: do-it-yourself

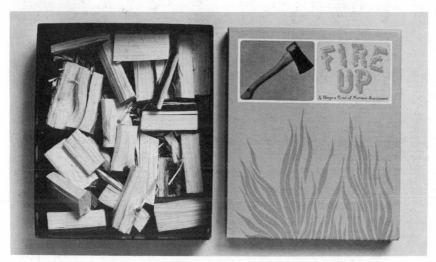

FIRE UP
& Blaze a Trail of Furnace Successes

SCE

Advertising is the voice of free choice!

Figure 36. *Above:* A piece that sells the idea that free choice is indispensable to the American way of life. Design: Gollin and Bright. Agency: Fletcher Richards Calkins & Holden. Photographer: Peter James Samerjan. *Opposite:* The double paper clip suggests the initial letters of the client and is a mark easily remembered. Client: Mel Whitson Stationers Inc. Design: Robert J. Overby.

Recently developed interest on the part of "city beautiful" groups is often focused on an attack on billboards as major contributors to the general ugliness of the cityscape. This attack has resulted in a re-evaluation of the function of the billboard, a new examination of its role in informing the public, and a new look at possibilities as to its structure.

Interestingly enough, the form of the billboard has not changed materially in a great many years. Why this should be is an interesting question. A few experiments were conducted at isolated points, mostly in Europe, by such firms as the Olivetti Corporation in Italy, who constructed a three-dimensional scaffolding that supported a variety of lettered panels of different proportions and colors. But such examples are rare. However, outdoor advertising is in a much more dynamic posture now than at any time in the past several years, if not decades. There will certainly be emphasis on better appearance as an outgrowth of a maturing culture and as a result of pressure from those groups interested in a more beautiful country. Leaders in the field of outdoor advertising have proposed a working partnership between architects and planners and the advertising industry. This proposal is part of a long-range program that may lead to forms of advertising that are integrated naturally into the fabric of our culture.

STATEMENT		Mel Whitson Stationers, Inc.	246 South Western Avenue, Los Angeles 4, California
■		■	
To		Telephone 388-2326	
■		■	

Mail upper portion with check and retain lower portion for your records

Mel Whitson Stationers, Inc.

Date	Invoice number	Charges	Credits	Balance

Figure 37. A happy symbol and a strong pattern of light and dark make this a selling poster as well as a carton. The lettering is appropriate in size and weight for the function of the package. Client: Devine's Dairy, East Norwalk, Conn. Design: Bill Wayman of Trinkhaus Aron & Wayman, Inc.

7

Packaging

The function of the package is to contain and protect the contents, keep food fresh, powder dry, liquids wet, make handling and shelf stocking simple and easy—and sell the product. In the face of considerable competition the package on the dealer's shelf must attract your attention, convince you in a second or two that the contents are what you really want (fresh, strong, pure, tasty, mild, safe, crisp, or whatever) and make you reach for it. All the other containers on the shelves are calling for attention too; so the one that succeeds, if the prices are similar, is the one that is most convincing and visually appealing.

The designer must create a visual symbol that projects the correct image of the product to the potential consumer. This may be accomplished through full-color photographic realism, poster-like abstraction, or a combination of the two. There is no hard and fast rule as each problem defines its own solution. The best designers get to the heart of the matter and develop clear, direct, and seemingly simple designs that are easy to remember and appropriate for the product involved. These men and women are aware of the preferences of the consumer as well as his tastes, buying habits, and psychological reactions to color, form, texture, and symbols in both product and package.

The design of the package is influenced not only by the ability of the designer but also by the many restrictions imposed on him by his client (budget, timetable, preferred colors, shapes or materials, and inclusion of additional text or "special 10 cents off" information) and by legal restrictions regarding size of type and required information as to weight, volume, and so forth.

The fact that the package is right in front of the buyer at the moment he makes up his mind suggests that it is the final argument in the sales campaign. Posters, newspapers, magazine, and television advertising have built an image or an idea in the mind of the potential

Figure 38. *Above:* Here white dominates for cleanliness with a fresh red rose for love and affection. The two combine to create a memorable image. Client: White King. Design: Jerome Gould Associates, Inc. *Right:* Low key lighting in taverns and bars makes a distinctive shape important in a package. The label plays a secondary role to the unusual form of the bottle. Client: Anheuser-Busch Inc. Design: Jerome Gould. *Opposite top:* The red, white, and blue of the French flag are used in this bold design. The letters are black. Client: Parisian Bakeries, San Francisco. Agency: Freeman & Gossage, Inc. Design: Marget Larson. *Opposite bottom:* A new bright plastic-coated boxboard was chosen for use in this carton. Colors are bright and cheerful suggesting health and fun. Client: Edgemont Farms. Design: Jerome Gould Associates, Inc.

Figure 39. *Above:* A new concept was attempted in this package—a container good looking enough to keep in the open within easy reach, nonrusting, nonslipping even with wet hands. Blow-molded polyethylene in a tapered oval form was the answer. Client: Boraxo. Design: Jerome Gould Associates, Inc. *Right:* Colorful, decorative and posterish, this container makes the purchase of a quart of milk a happy event. Client: Taylor's Dairy, Inc., Jenkintown, Pa. Design: Mel Richman/Sam Ciccone.

consumer which must be correlated with the design of the packages and containers. The package thus becomes the final phase of a series of inroads on the resistance or lack of interest on the part of the consumer.

In order to keep looking up to date and reflect recent developments in taste as well as indicating the improvements in the characteristics of the product, the package designer must periodically redo the design. The number of sales people employed by individual retail stores is decreasing; therefore the package must also be a silent salesman, looking attractive enough to confirm in the customer's mind his desire to buy.

The success of the package lies, however, not in the initial sale, important as that may be, but in the actions of the buyer after that first package has been emptied. It is on the basis of the continuity of repeat sales that the manufacturer is able to survive and earn a profit. Although motivational researchers have stressed the "irrational" in the act of buying, it is precisely at this point that the customer should have an opportunity, as Saul Bass put it, "to exercise rational behavior if she chooses to do so." The "wants" of people, rational or not, should not be the only concern of the manufacturer. He should also consider what they "need." Information is required that gives the housewife a fair opportunity to easily compare the prices of competing products according to standards of size and weight; descriptions that have some semblance of meaning should replace such terms as "giant," "family," "economy," "jumbo," "large"; a system should be used that gives more precision to the meaning of such terms as "serves six" or "four washer loads."

Because the package will probably be shown endless numbers of times on television there must be consideration for its ability to "read" well on the screen, both in color and in black and white. Pretesting over closed-circuit television is being used to determine the visual effect of the package and estimate the probable impact of the design when seen fleetingly in commercials of various lengths and types. All of the positive elements of the package can be utilized in TV selling: the easy-open fastener, the built-in pouring spout, the protective liner, the informative side panels.

Belatedly recognized as a serious problem is the final disposition of the container. Not only should we be well aware of the esthetics, utility, and possible related use of the package; we should also consider its eventual disposal. As things are now, some 90 millions of tons of garbage and trash must be disposed of annually. As a result of our lack of planning we have quickly polluted our atmosphere, streams, and beaches. Much of this refuse will not burn, cannot be converted

Figure 40. *Above:* An imported Danish crispbread is crisply packaged in a fold-up box making good use of photography and patterns of Viking ships. Client: Copenhagen Crispbread Factory Ltd. Design: Vance Jonson. *Right:* A beer bottle and its label form an integrated whole in a smooth simple shape. Client: Carlsberg. Design: Richard C. Runyon. *Opposite top:* Excellent use of photography to show the happy, healthy "consumers." There is no "front" or "back" as the package reads well from all directions. Client: Hap Pet Food Co. Design: Vance Jonson. *Opposite bottom:* The friendly mutt on the label of this can of dog food suggests a friendly product. The shield form framing the dog's face is used on products of this company. Client: Hap Pet Food Co. Design: Vance Jonson.

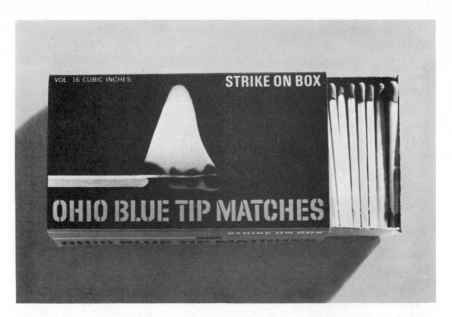

Figure 41. *Top:* The burning match shows the product with great clarity and simplicity. Client: Ohio Blue Tip Matches. Design: Saul Bass & Assoc. *Above:* The label, carton, and display all follow the same posterish idea. Client: Artone Studio India Ink/H. M. Storms. Design: Push Pin Studios, Inc. *Right:* Almost like wrapping a loaf of bread in a newspaper, this design includes in the "news" recipes, the price and information about the bread. Client: Di Carlo's Baking Co., San Pedro, Calif. Design: Saul Bass. *Opposite:* A new product identity was required suggesting quality. The square jars resist toppling and display well. Colors are rich and warm. Client: House of Herbs, Inc. Art Director: Lester Beall. Design: Lester Beall, Inc./Clifford Stead, Jr.

into usable fertilizer, and can no longer be foisted off on smaller communities in the guise of "fill" for unused valleys and ravines.

The mountain of material left over daily in rubbish bins and garbage cans indicates that a very high standard of living is currently being enjoyed by most Americans. We had better, however, give thought to the development of containers for our goods and food products that lend themselves readily to some civilized method of disposal. After all, a hot-dog bun is consumed along with the weenie, as is the cone with the ice cream, the bun with the hamburger. Edible packaging for foods with a disposable outer wrap that melts in warm water (like the plastic pouches containing soap or bleach now on the market) may answer part of this problem.

The national bill for garbage collection is now something like 3 billion dollars annually. Obviously some meaningful creative thinking had better be done—and soon. Reconstructing waste materials and rubbish into building materials might be another approach to their use, if not their disposal. Could we use waste plastic bottles, foam coffee cups, and cardboard shipping containers as the raw ingredients for a new type of wall panel for houses and offices? Could empty milk cartons begin life anew as closet doors, or might no-return plastic beer bottles reincarnate themselves as a new type of resilient flooring?

The Office of Solid Wastes has been created within the Public Health Service to deal with the general problem of discovering what to do with the 8 billion pounds of solid trash our society dumps in vacant lots and along our highways every year. This new office estimates that within twenty years we will be producing and discarding three times as much rubbish (24 billion pounds). This fantastic quantity of material has to go somewhere, some of it as fertilizer perhaps, the rest in ceramics or building materials or for some other similar use. Clearly there exists a problem, solutions to which must be found before we are buried in our own refuse.

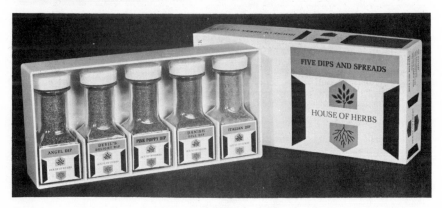

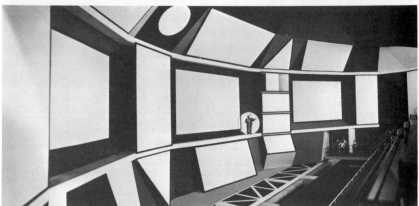

Figure 42. The interior of the ovoid theater of the IBM exhibit at the New York World Fair of 1964-65 contained a multiplicity of screens. The complexity was intentional, so the viewer would never be certain from where the information would come next. Slides and motion pictures were synchronized with the appearance of a commentator who popped up at several different locations during the showing. On the screens at the moment are examples of the "twoness" of things. Client: International Business Machines Corp. Design: Charles Eames.

8

Exhibition Design

Exhibition design is involved with two problems: content and structure. The content is the meaning of the message or the theme of the exhibit—what the show has to say. The structure is the physical construction that carries the message—poles, panels, beams, frames, cases. It is probable that the best exhibition designers come from the ranks of graphic designers, as these are the people who are primarily concerned with communicating a message. To them the structure is of practical interest but is, at the same time, of strictly secondary importance.

The industrial designer who gets involved in exhibition work sometimes tends to give undue emphasis to the construction because that is the part of the whole job that appeals most strongly to him. He is often structure-oriented rather than message-oriented. This generalization must, of course, be taken for what it is—a generalization that is challenged by a number of notable exceptions.

Many of the interesting structures at recent world fairs contained displays that were far less interesting than the buildings themselves. Some of these consisted of well-placed panels, well lighted, wonderfully colored, and covered with lettering from top to bottom. Each panel contained enough words to fill a chapter and, often, the panel was situated so that it could be seen only by people who were passing it at a brisk walk if not almost at a dead run. No one could, much less would, stop and stand in front of the message and deliberately read all the information it contained even if it had been interesting—which was not often the case.

A few words in a clean typeface of reasonable size would have been seen, read, and understood and, perhaps, even remembered. A tendency to get "wordy" spoiled many otherwise well-thought-out exhibits. It is questionable just how much information a visitor takes away

Figure 43. An exhibition devoted to the life of Nehru as it was erected for a showing in Los Angeles, 1966. Large photographs, actual objects, records, mementos, and works of art were arranged on panels as islands around which the spectators walked. The many sections were capable of being grouped in several ways to accommodate the exhibition in a variety of different sizes and shapes of rooms. Client: Government of India. Design: Charles Eames.

with him anyway. Some of the most successful of the exhibits at the same fairs stressed the spoken word (rather than the written), where an idea could be explained and developed while the spectator was engrossed in the visual aspects of the presentation. A quiet voice murmuring in your ear, telling you simply and directly what it is you are seeing, informs without boring or irritating—or forcing you to read quantities of material of little interest.

In the case of a major fair, where the average visitor does a great deal of walking, a simple thing like aching feet may well prevent him from paying very close attention. He may not visit an exhibit at all if it means walking another quarter of a mile. Putting the visitor in a chair or seat that moves at a controlled speed through an exhibit while the show goes on all around him is to treat him like the important person he is. The entire fair exists for his benefit, for him to see and absorb and be influenced by. Treating him as a VIP is only common courtesy—and may be good business too.

Some of the really notable exhibits at these fairs did just that. They took into account the fatigue factor and made viewing pleasant for the spectator once he entered their structures. The mobs of people who were forced to wait for long periods in lengthy lines before being able to get inside is, however, another matter. One fine day the major exhibitions will provide a continuous chair-ride through all the best exhibits with opportunities to get on or off at several points along the way. In this event the exterior structure may prove to be of less importance as an eye-catching feature. One huge geodesic dome could easily cover the entire fair, could at a minimum cover the major exhibitors areas and make a continuous ride-through a simple matter technically and one that is most exciting for the viewer.

General Motors provided such a ride at their exhibitions at the New York fairs of 1939 and 1964. The spectator sat in a comfortable chair and was moved along a series of views of the world of tomorrow as a voice in his ear informed him of the details. Several other firms provided similar experiences for those who viewed their exhibits, although the G.M. presentation was probably the most extensive and detailed.

Some of the most successful exhibits are small, simple, and effective. No spectaculars, no fireworks. Just clear entertaining information. Denmark has a habit of producing a clean, colorful, understandable exhibit usually stressing the quality of Danish goods. Sweden provides cool, crystalline, restrained design that always attracts favorable attention.

Film is now an important part of many exhibitions. A film is a problem in design every bit as much as the room in which it will be shown. Most films produced to be shown as part of an exhibition

Figure 44. *Above:* The Los Angeles Art Directors annual exhibition is a harrowing affair for those who must design and install it. By using a simple wood batten attached to the floor and ceiling with wire stretched between, the graphic material could seemingly float unsupported in space. Small electric terminals were crimped to the wires and a brass notebook fastener pushed through punched holes in the illustration and the eyeholes of the terminals. This system was the least expensive ever used and one of the most pleasing esthetically. Client: Los Angeles Art Directors Club. Design: Louis Danziger. Photo-

88

graph: Marvin Rand. *Above:* Since the average exhibit viewer does not stop long enough to absorb detailed information, the School of Design at Ulm, Germany, used photographs enlarged to 46 by 69 inches mounted on slightly curved sheets of metal which could then be set up without having to be fastened to the floor. A 23-inch-high sheet metal base lifted the photos to eye level. When completed the exhibit formed a half circle and was completely stable. Exhibit used at the Triennale di Milano, 1960. Client: Hochschule fur Gestaltung, Ulm, Germany. Design: Herbert Ohl and Claus Wille.

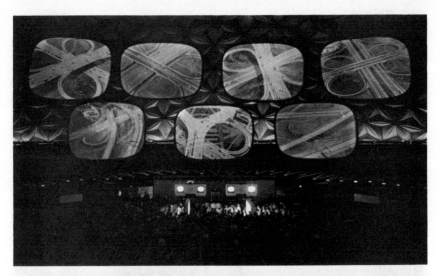

Figure 45. *Top:* Part of the American exhibition in Sokolniki Park, Moscow, 1959, was housed in a geodesic dome. Seven huge screens were arranged in two rows onto which were projected some two thousand images of American life in a twelve-minute show. Shopping centers, traffic jams, homes, highways, and the like were shown in a very believable manner. Client: U.S. Government. Design: Charles Eames. *Bottom:* A collage technique crowds a great deal of material on printing into a small space. The text is on a wall by itself. Client: London Master Printers Assoc. Design: Crosby/Fletcher/Forbes/Gill. *Opposite:* Draping his forms in giant sweeps from ceiling to floor, accentuating the drama of the sweep with lighting at floor level, the designer was able to use many of the large surfaces as backgrounds for photographs, drawings, or lettering. Client: "Projections" exhibit. Design: Michael Lax.

90

Figure 46. The multiple-screen technique used in the Science building at the Seattle Fair of 1962 began with one projected image of
a structure "housing" science that grew into a second image and a
third until all six images filled the wall with fanciful architecture.
The film continued to tell the story through six synchronized images
as the spectators sat on the floor in a most relaxed way, enjoying both
the film and the opportunity to sit down. Client: U.S. Government.
Design: Charles Eames.

are rather mediocre attempts to glamorize the product or overdramatize it. The best films stem from top designers who have been given an assignment and relatively free hand, at least as to the general approach. Whether the budget is large or small is of less importance than the amount of imagination and resourcefulness of the designer involved.

A film to be shown to a large audience requires a room that can be blacked-out. A film to be shown to one person or a small group can be run in a room with fairly normal lighting through the use of a machine that projects the image on the screen from the rear. Such a back-projection system can be put into operation by the spectator, who needs only to push a button. Short explanatory films can present the operation of a scientific principle, a mechanism, or a series of facts in a manner that entertains while it instructs.

Movement through an exhibition can be controlled to a precise degree by the manner in which the exhibit is designed. Some are organized into a linear path along which the spectator moves, receiving information in a chronological order or in a predetermined sequence. In other cases a completely free flow of traffic in all directions may be more desirable, permitting the viewer to see the things he wishes and ignore those he prefers to omit. The latter method often takes the form of "islands" of panels or objects around which free movement is allowed. If the subject of the exhibition permits, breaking the total information down into digestible sections and letting each section stand alone, an island type of display results quite naturally.

Many exhibitions contain both isolated bits of information and quantities of material best absorbed in a particular order. The solid wall surfaces of the exhibition room may form the background for the each-item-in-order section of the show, while the center of the room may be reserved for individual segments arranged as island areas.

"White piqué is an innocent fabric. I wanted to shape it into a strict, straight, dress in which a lady could slither and glide."

Anne Fogarty

Zepel stain protected piqué of 65% Dacron polyester and 35% cotton.   Sizes 4 to 14. $30. At stores listed on page 000.

Figure 47. A disarmingly simple dress that uses one long ruffle to accentuate the length of the dress and, in its casual placement, eliminates the need for any other adornment. Client: Anne Fogarty. Design: Anne Fogarty. Advertisement: Leonard Sacks. Art Director: Mel Platt. Photographer: Ira Maser.

9

Fashion

Fashion is a strange world where *design* is restricted to a "look" rather than a functional element of primary importance. Most of the people engaged in fashion styling seem to feel that the human body is somehow all wrong—and it is their job to correct it, now one way, now another. Human proportions have not materially changed throughout history, yet those proportions (and the human form itself) apparently require revamping each season. One suspects the real underlying reason to be a desire to sell still more clothing to people who have closets full of perfectly usable apparel already. To convince these potential customers they need new clothes, the clothing industry must make them ashamed of and dissatisfied with their "old" clothes.

The notion then develops that it is preferable to make any sacrifice rather than be seen in clothing no longer fashionable. A person can be taught to feel very uncomfortable in well-fitted comfortable clothing if a lapel is too broad (or narrow), if a cuff is too large (or small), if a color is "last year's" rather than that currently in vogue. Real comfort is rarely of any interest to the stylist. His problems are only peripherally functional ones. He deals in trivia like length of hem, shape of neckline, size of pocket. Some few, however, eschew construction that gives an artificial shape to the person wearing the garment. The clothing developed by these designers depends on the body of the wearer to create the proper look and fit. Those who buy and wear clothing by these designers usually fit into a type—conscious of the body and its fitness, quite aware how they look, and aware of the fact that the clothing of one particular designer is most appropriate for them. They are often people with considerable knowledge about design and how to make it work for them.

Fashion is not based on logic, unless it is the odd logic of the illogical. That is, fashion is not an attempt, like product design or

Figure 48. *Above left:* An advertisement for a sportswear manufacturer that includes a large number of items well placed in relation to one another. Client: Rose Marie Reid. Agency: Carson/Roberts. *Above right:* The strong brush technique of the harem skirt contrasts with the fine line detail in the beaded bodice. A Helen Rose dress. Client: Robinson's, Los Angeles. Artist: Ellen Van Buren. *Opposite:* In a series of advertisements saluting young designers the May Co. in Los Angeles used art work that was crisp and strong. These two ads were especially effective and the clothing shown was well designed —even well engineered. Client: May Co., Los Angeles. Design: Staff Artists.

May Co Salutes American Young Designers

"I define my look in simple, wearable, 'today' kind of clothes," says Leo Narducci. "I don't design for a model because the women who wear them will have different proportions. My designs are young, but I don't put an age on them . . . they're for everyone over 18!" May Co endorses Leo Narducci's design for eternal youth.

Leo Narducci

From Leo Narducci of Guy D: Blinding print on silk.
burnoose shift; lilac-gold-black. $5.98
Criss-sleeved beach dress of pure Irish linen; white appliquéd in rings of color. $5.98
Sizes 6-14.
may co cosmopolitan dresses 96—all thirteen stores

DOWNTOWN • WILSHIRE • CRENSHAW • LAKEWOOD • VALLEY
EASTLAND • SOUTH BAY • SAN DIEGO • BUENA PARK • TOPANGA PLAZA
WEST LOS ANGELES • WHITTIER • SOUTH COAST PLAZA

MAY CO
CALIFORNIA

May Co Salutes American Young Designers

"I design for the woman who feels there is more effect in a simple dress than one where there's a lot happening," says Dominique. "Because of my background in math and physics, I approach design as an engineer. A dress or suit should hang from the shoulders in fabrics with moldability . . . and when the woman wears it, it moves and flows as she walks . . . as part of her personality." May Co goes with Dominique into new fashion frontiers.

From Dominique Jones for Dominique:
Left: The 'butterfly wing,' a late-day dress in fully-lined rayon-acetate crepe. Tiger lily orange; 6 to 14. $42.00
Right: Day dress in pure silk, with midrif ingot-ting. Cherry lim; 8 to 14. $32.00
may co forecast dresses 22—all thirteen stores

DOWNTOWN—WILSHIRE—CRENSHAW—LAKEWOOD
VALLEY—EASTLAND—WEST L.A.—SOUTH BAY
SAN DIEGO—BUENA PARK—TOPANGA PLAZA
WHITTIER—SOUTH COAST PLAZA

MAY CO
CALIFORNIA

97

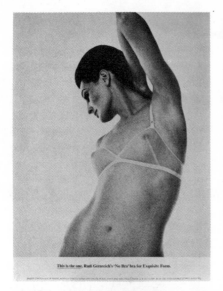

Figure 49. *Top left:* An excellent example of the tasteful use of the human form in photography emphasized through soft lighting and a grainy print. Client: Exquisite Form. Agency: Papert Koenig Lois, Inc. Art Director: Ralph Tuzzo. Photographer: Ted Vendikos. Bra design: Rudi Gernreich. *Top right:* Swimsuit with narrow bib front, 1963. Design: Rudi Gernreich. Photo: Margaret Townsend. *Bottom left:* Tunic dress with cloche hat/mask and gloves, 1964. Design: Rudi Gernreich. Photo: William Claxton. *Bottom right:* Transparent shirt with low dark collar, 1964. Design: Rudi Gernreich. Photo: William Claxton.

packaging, to solve an actual design problem. Clothing that is intended to solve a functional problem, like the space suit of the astronaut or the protective garb of the fire fighter, is in another category altogether. Fashion is an unceasing attempt to continually make women, and to an increasing extent men, look different enough from the way they had just looked to satisfy the artificially induced need they have now accepted. THE look is a constantly changing affair. Of necessity, it must be.

Those who give leadership and direction to fashion are men, often youngish men, who have strong ideas as to how women should look. These ideas change and develop over the years, but usually the general vision remains. Strong geometric simplicity or soft-flowing ethereal translucency, the mark of the individual designer, is often so strong that his work can easily be identified as his own from its general appearance.

Occasionally a long-term trend is understood well enough to make some predictions possible. A case in point was the women's topless swim suit brought forth a bit prematurely by Rudi Gernreich owing to pressure from buyers who had heard his prediction that this change was about due and should occur within a very few years. Shock, outrage, and anguished objections arose at once, but too late to change the situation. Cocktail waitresses and entertainers in topless attire sprang up on all sides, indicating that the topless idea had been waiting in the wings to make its appearance just as Gernreich, and others, had known.

Fashion, which is not terribly interesting at the moment despite obvious current trends, may become so if we can believe the predictions of the psychologists who have investigated the reasons man has given for the wearing of clothing. There is a fairly unanimous opinion that the original reason for man's adorning himself was a desire for more spectacular decoration than a scraggly beard. Perhaps man, lacking colorful feathers or a thick fur hide, felt somewhat inadequate. At any rate his first reason for covering his body was clearly a decorative one.

Protection from the weather might be advanced as another major reason for the wearing of garments. However much of the world is pleasant enough, at least part of the year; much of it is fine all year 'round; and yet some sort of clothing was developed and worn even under ideal climatic conditions. In very unpleasant climes, however, there have been those, like the Patagonians, who decorated themselves but never bothered to protect themselves against the cold with clothing.

Protection of one's reproductive organs from the magic of the evil eye of one's enemies is a more logical (?)—or should we say, more

Figure 50. *Above left:* A short tube dress of perforated vinyl with punched-out vinyl on legs, hands, and face as decorations. 196__. Design: Rudi Gernreich. Photo: Tommy Mitchell. *Above right:* Short kimono-like dress. 196__. Design: Rudi Gernreich. Photo: Tommy Mitchell. *Opposite left:* Short dress with bulky sleeves, wrap belt, worn with knee-length boots, 1965. Design: Rudi Gernreich. Photo: William Claxton. *Opposite right:* Short dark dress with one stripe down one side continuing as a stripe down the stocking, 1965. Design: Rudi Gernreich. Photo: Tommy Mitchell. The series of de-

signs by Rudi Gernreich illustrates the variety of expression possible while following one main concept. This designer is well known for his avant-garde ideas, often followed a year or two later by others in the fashion field who adapt or alter his ideas without understanding his motivation or direction. Several examples are shown, not because he is typical of the field but rather because he has shown himself to be more imaginative and inventive than most of his competition and his work has been more predictive.

Figure 51. *Above:* A wool dress with a turtle-neck top, plain skirt with matching kid belt and shoes. Source: Buffum's, Long Beach. Photo: Tommy Mitchell.

likely—idea. A belief in the power of witchcraft has not yet died and
many methods have been developed to protect one from its effects.
Concealment is one technique that has long been used—with no apparent effect, of course. But we are still using it.

Modesty is the third reason usually advanced to explain the
existence of clothing. The facts would indicate the exact opposite is
more likely to be the case. Rather than concealing the body in an
attempt to be modest, clothing is more often used to permit partial
revealment of one's charms. The nude human body may be anything
from beautiful to ugly. The one thing it is *not* is erotically exciting.
Partial revealment through glimpses of areas usually kept covered
is an ancient technique for attracting the interest of the observer.
Without clothing of some sort this cannot be done. So rather than
"modesty" we might suggest "erotic attraction" as a more honest
term to employ.

As we continue to air-condition our dwellings, places of work,
vehicles, and the like, we lose "protection" as a reason for continuing
to wear clothing. We spend more and more time in a conditioned
environment and less and less actually exposed to the elements. It is
quite possible for a man to live many weeks without having physically
to expose himself to the weather. One man in New York tested this
idea. He left his air-conditioned apartment in the morning, took the
elevator to the basement garage, got into his air-conditioned car, drove
to his office building, parked in the basement garage, took an elevator
to his office, worked, had lunch in a restaurant in a connecting building, reversed the order in returning home in the late afternoon. He
found he could attend the theater, do much of his shopping, and so
forth without ever truly being "outside." The point here is that protection as a reason for the existence of clothing gets increasingly weaker
and may soon cease altogether.

Modesty is whatever a culture decides it is. The rules change
from one country to another, even from one time of day to another.
It depends on the situation, the people involved, the circumstances. It
is a tricky business and defies clear description. What is modest here
and now may be silly an hour later. The whole procedure is too
whimsical to take seriously. And it continually changes. What was
modest for grandmother in her youth is quaintly ridiculous today. And
tomorrow, what?

Decoration remains the only reason for the wearing of *something*.
The first reason may well become the final surviving reason. Naked
human beings are not too often an esthetic sight. Even the best proportioned humans in good physical condition may, like the caveman,
benefit from the addition of some sort of decoration.

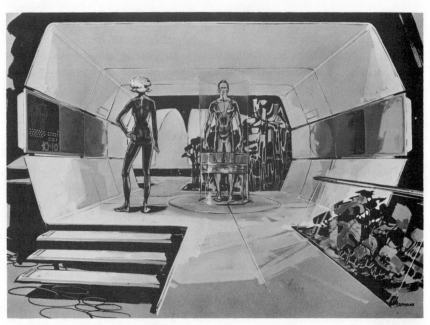

The new "clothing" then may more likely be purely decorative material such as paint (in a variety of patterns and colors, easily changed to suit the occasion), "glued-on" jewels, ornaments, sequins, ribbons, or strings of sparklers (baubles, bangles, and beads). Fabrics may still be used but in quite different ways. Translucent materials could give the body mystery and allure, the body itself decorated top to toe with fluorescent color, changing patterns in different lighting situations. This leopard could change her spots merely by turning to face a different light.

The whole concept of decorating people rather than clothing them leads to an altogether new approach and manner of thinking. One of the functions of clothing, the psychologists tell us, is to make each sex more attractive to the other. Except in rare instances we are doing an exceptionally poor job of it. The typical daily garb of average men and women reduces them to the status of worker bees, neither queen nor warrior—just neuter gender. Perhaps we could not stand the emotional strain of being so continually aware of the other sex if we stressed the differences between the sexes through attractive decoration. But some day soon we will find ourselves trying it anyway.

Figure 52. *Opposite:* If protection from the weather and modesty (a changeable factor to say the least) are dispensed with as reasons for wearing clothing, we are left with pure decoration as the sole remaining reason. Decoration becomes "people decoration" and calls for a whole new orientation. Given sufficient time to develop, an entirely new method of "dressing" could develop in which the body would not need to be covered to protect it from the gaze of others— at least not covered with fabric. The young designer who created the illustrations shown here took a new direction, suggesting a method using a scanning device that would project a pattern directly onto the body, then spray a film onto the person that would retain the pattern in colors selected ahead of time. A dissolving spray would remove the "clothing" and cycle the material for re-use. New body decorations are thus available at a moment's notice with esthetic effects not possible today. The necessity for clothing storage, cleaning, maintenance, and such would be eliminated, and a tremendous "wardrobe" would be available in one small reel of tape for the scanner. (Circa 2015.) Design: Julius John Cassani. Photo: John J. Krawczyk.

Figure 53. Leaving some of the areas of a drawing in an unfinished state draws attention to those areas that have been treated more completely. The viewer has an opportunity to complete the drawing in his own imagination. Artist: Roy Alexander.

10

Illustration

There was a time when the artist-illustrator had things pretty much his own way. If an event was to be visualized at all, it was the imagination and creative skill of the artist that made the picture possible. Products were advertised with words and pictures—the artist again making it possible to see what the product looked like. Historical events were pictured so the public could understand how the event happened. History was made visible.

Then photography was developed, made simpler, quicker, and cheaper. The lens viewed scenes in a manner most convincing. All the details were revealed, the drama captured—and it was fast. The daily newspapers capitalized on the ability of photography to show what had happened short hours after the event had occurred. Products could be seen exactly as they looked on the dealer's shelf. The artist was in trouble.

As the situation developed it was found that there was a need for both the artist-illustrator and the photoillustrator. The artist could picture things that had not yet happened, he could show events, places and ideas that could not readily be photographed. The photographer, however, could reveal with great exactitude the appearance of an object, the character of a person, or the details of an event, and could interpret and create as well as record.

Good illustration is based on the discipline of good drawing. Solid draftsmanship permits the artist to give graphic expression to situations that will hold the viewer's attention, awake an emotional response, interest his intellect. The artist must develop his ability to visualize, invent, interpret, and organize visual elements into a comprehensive whole. His work, like that of any artist, takes on a particular character, a "look" that identifies the work as his own. He must have the kind

Figure 54. *Top:* A two-page illustration for a science fiction magazine story by Philip Wylie. The strength of the art work reflects the grim power of the story. Client: *Saturday Evening Post.* Artist: Neil Boyle. *Bottom:* Note the manner in which the layout provided for the center fold of the magazine. Client: *Good Housekeeping.* Artist: John Asaro. *Opposite top:* A portfolio piece suggesting a story. Artist: Park Merrill. *Opposite bottom:* Direct and simple means can accomplish a good deal. Artist: Roy Alexander.

Figure 55. *Top:* A portfolio piece suggesting the idea of flight. Artist: Park Merrill. *Bottom:* An artist's recording of the recovery of capsule Discovery XIV off Honolulu, 1960. The use of silhouetted figures is most effective. Client: U.S. Government. Artist: Ren Wicks.

illustration   111

of empathy that enables him to reveal through his work the intent and concept of the author or the art director.

To achieve the desired authenticity the illustrator depends on accurate and complete research. He must develop a knowledge of the location and character of sources of information, especially pictorial information. He usually develops an extensive file of magazine and newspaper clippings, photographs of a tremendous variety of objects, incidents, places, costumes, architecture, vehicles, and the like.

Through his manner of handling pencil, chalk, ink, or paint the illustrator can impart the character he wishes to the work he creates. It might be dark and moody or bright and sparkling. The viewer receives a direct clue to the nature of the story or the direction of the advertisement through his first glimpse of the nature of the illustration. The art director or editor selects a particular artist because of his past performance—his style. His work is intended to complement the work of the other people involved in the production of the advertisement or the design of the magazine page. The illustrator usually works as a member of a team—a creative team—as it requires the integrated efforts of several kinds of talent and ability to organize, lay out, compose, and arrange an advertisement, a brochure, a magazine, or a book. The style of the illustration must be consistent with the general concept and the message carried by the text. Art as pure self-expression is not relevant here.

Today's illustrator has come very close in his approach to his assignments to that of the "fine artist"—the painter. He works in many media—oil on canvas, tempera, water color, collage, and combinations of these. Many illustrations in the leading women's magazines, notably *McCall's, Saturday Evening Post* and *Ladies Home Journal,* are of such quality and esthetic merit that the originals could well be framed and hung on the wall—and they often are. One can only speculate as to the time art enthusiasts discover this rich vein and begin bidding for an original Bernie Fuchs, David Stone Martin, Austin Briggs, or Barbara Robinson.

The magazines just mentioned were a few years ago among those looking rather dull and pedestrian. Readers began looking elsewhere for more visual excitement, and the magazines reacted by introducing a redesign program that changed their appearance and outlook in short order. Fresh design and a new kind of illustration appeared that not only brought back former readers but attracted new ones as well. Fine illustrations persuaded housewives to take time out to read the short novel and lengthy short story each issue brought them. Articles on interesting subjects were made doubly so by the fresh interpretations of the illustrators.

Figure 56. *Above:* A piece intended expressly for the artist's port-folio. Artist: John Asaro. *Opposite:* Another portfolio piece suggesting the beginning of a boy-girl relationship. Artist: Park Merrill.

Figure 57. *Above:* A dramatic study in tones of gray. The rough texturing suggests the strength and dynamics of large aircraft. Artist: Richard Harvey. *Right:* A portfolio piece to demonstrate technical ability and to indicate the artist's accuracy in handling reference material to complete the proper details of furnishing and decor. Artist: Neil Boyle.

illustration   **115**

The main difference between illustrators and "fine artists" lies in their emotional attitude toward their work. A can of beer rendered by a good illustrator would look frosty, inviting, and tempting regardless of the artist's feelings about beer. Even if he cordially disliked beer his work would never reflect this fact. However, it is precisely the painter's *feeling* about the subject that motivates him. If *he* disliked beer and was moved to create a painting about his feelings the can might be rusty, dented, peeling, and seen on top of a litter pile mixed with garbage. His emotions would motivate him in the first place and rule what he had to say about the subject.

The illustrator's work is intended to motivate someone to buy a product or read a story. The painter's work is intended to make a statement about something that can speak to people for a long long time. The good illustrator puts more into his work than the client realizes, in the sense that much of his work relates in its possible lasting qualities to serious painting. For example, the ceiling of the Sistine chapel was simply an illustration assignment, but the final product has brought people thousands of miles to see it for a great many years.

Many illustrators have become quite good photographers as they have had to photograph people, places, and things as resource material for their work. These photographs, along with clippings from magazines and newspapers, are called "scrap" (as in *scrapbook*) and are referred to in order to obtain accuracy of detail in the creation of an illustration. And, along with some skill with a camera, the illustrator needs considerable background in the so-called academic areas. He must know something about economics, history, psychology, and other fields in order to have the depth and breadth of understanding required for any creative work. The technical skill required can be learned by practice and hard work, but the material needed by the imagination must be furnished through study of man and his works. This is not unique among illustrators; it is generally true of all the people whose work is shown in this book, regardless of the specialized area in which they might work.

It is possibly this overall need for background and enrichment that has led the best of today's illustrators to a more serious study of the work of the old masters. Not only their techniques, but their attitudes and approaches to their work are of interest to men working in today's world. Times have changed enormously, but some attitudes remain constant. A man's enjoyment of his work, his delight in being able to do a workman-like job, solving a difficult problem in a new and superior way—these remain.

Figure 58. An economical study in tones of gray with only the essentials shown. Artist: Dave Plourde.

bibliography

BOOKS

Annual of Advertising and Editorial Art and Design. New York: Art Directors Club of America.

BARR, ALFRED H., JR., *De Stijl.* New York: Museum of Modern Art, 1961.

BLAKE, PETER, *God's Own Junkyard.* New York: Holt, Rinehart and Winston, Inc., 1964.

DREXLER, ARTHUR, *Ludwig Mies van der Rohe.* New York: George Braziller, Inc., 1960.

FLETCHER, ALAN; FORBES, COLIN; and GILL, BOB, *Graphic Design: Visual Comparisons.* New York: Reinhold Publishing Corporation, 1963.

FRANCK, KLAUS, *Exhibitions.* London: The Architectural Press, Ltd., 1961.

FULLER, BUCKMINSTER, *Ideas and Integrities.* Englewood Cliffs, N.J.: Prentice-Hall, Inc., 1963.

GROPIUS, WALTER and ISE, *Bauhaus,* 1919-1928, ed. Herbert Bayer, 2nd printing, Boston: Charles T. Branford Company, 1952.

HATJE, GERD and URSULA, *Design for Living.* New York: Harry N. Abrams, Inc., 1962.

KAUFMAN, EDGAR, JR., *What Is Modern Design?* New York: Museum of Modern Art, 1950.

LEWIS, JOHN, *Typography: Basic Principles.* New York: Reinhold Publishing Corporation, 1963.

MARKS, ROBERT, *The Dymaxion World of Buckminster Fuller.* New York: Reinhold Publishing Corporation, 1960.

MOHOLY-NAGY, L., *Vision in Motion.* Chicago: Paul Theobald, 1947.

MÜLLER-BROCKMAN, J., *The Graphic Artist and His Design Problems.* Arthur Niggli, 1961; Hastings House Publishers, 1961.

NELSON, GEORGE, *Display.* New York: Whitney Publications, Inc., 1953.

RUDOFSKY, BERNARD, *Are Clothes Modern?* Chicago: P. Theobald & Co., Publishers, 1947.

117

SUTTON, JAMES, *Signs in Action.* New York: Reinhold Publishing Corporation, 1965.

WEIHS, KURT, and STRUNSKY, ROBERT, *The Visual Craft of William Golden,* ed. Cipe Pineless Golden. New York: George Braziller Inc., 1962.

PERIODICALS

Art Direction, 19 West 44th St., New York, N.Y. 10036.

Arts and Architecture, 3305 Wilshire Blvd., Los Angeles, California 90005.

CA Magazine, 3975 East Bayshore Road, Palo Alto, California 94303.

Design, 28, Haymarket, London, S.W. 1, England.

Domus, obtainable through European Publishers Representatives, Inc., 132 West 43rd Street, New York, N.Y. 10036.

Gebrauchsgraphik, obtainable through Overseas Publishers Representatives, 20 West 34th St., New York, N.Y. 10001.

Graphis, obtainable through Walter Herdeg, P.O. Box 320, New York, N.Y. 10005.

Industrial Design, Whitney Publications, Inc., 18 East 50th St., New York, N.Y. 10022.

Interiors, Whitney Publications, Inc., 18 East 50th St., New York, N.Y. 10022.

Mobilia, obtainable through W. Sorenson, 6311 Wilshire Blvd., Los Angeles, California 90048.

Print, 527 Madison Ave., New York, N.Y. 10022.

index